Walk In The Light

by Patti Hill

Original artwork of the escape from Romania commissioned by Charles and Linda Grisham of Wichita, Kansas.

Artist is Bob Ward of Mesa, Arizona.

Map is courtesy of Perry-Castaneda Library Map Collection, Library at the University of Texas at Austin and is a public domain map.

Map was obtained at http://www.lib.utexas.edu/maps/europe/romania-pol69.jpg

Further information about Charlie Duke, his life as an astronaut, his ministry, or for a copy of his book, *Moonwalker*, write to:

Duke Ministry for Christ
P.O. Box 310345
New Braunfels, TX 78131

All scripture references were taken from the NIV, NKJV, or KJV of the Bible.

Graphic Design & Typesetting by:
New Creations, 636-583-2324, or www.ncimpact.com

Editing & Proofreading by: Micki Goodell, mickigoodell@yahoo.com

Writing by: Patti Hill, hillwriter@yahoo.com

DEDICATION

I am dedicating this book to my precious wife, Aurica. Without her strength, support, and firm stand with me in ministry, this work would not be where it is today. She is truly my helpmate.

To my children: Fivi, Daniel, Marianne, Lidia, Samuel, Veronica, Benjamin, Jonathon, Betty, and our precious Iliuta. They have also stood shoulder to shoulder with me working on behalf of the children in Romania.

PREFACE

One of the reasons Dan and Amy hired me to run the Walk in the Light office was to help in writing this book. I was eager to take on the challenge of documenting Brother Ilie's testimony.

As we recorded him the first time he came to the United States, three things struck me:

1) Brother Ilie's style of speaking was so simple, direct, and down-to-earth that I didn't want to lose that element once we started writing. Indeed, the family wanted his voice to resonate from the pages.

2) As Brother Ilie finished many of his stories, I was impressed with the fact that there were biblical principles involved. From this came the development of a short section after most chapters that pulls together the principle and scripture references. Each of us will have the opportunity to apply these principles to our own life.

3) As we moved into our second round of recording, I began to wish I could ask Sister Aurica how she handled circumstances and challenges. I heard how Brother Ilie had dealt with happenings, but what was her perspective? What was it like to see her husband slip into the night and never return? What was it like to have him come home beaten and bloodied, yet powerless to stop the brutality of the secret police? These questions needed an answer, so we began to record Aurica as well. Her stories and perspective are sprinkled throughout.

We have done our best to provide a clear and accurate accounting of events. We hope that you not only enjoy the book, but that it will be used as a witnessing tool as well. We pray that God will use it mightily for His purposes.

Enjoy!

Patti

INTRODUCTION

Many of you have heard my stories told over the years. There was even a book written many years ago chronicling how God had used me and led me out of Romania. Many of these stories, while correct in spirit, weren't correct in every detail.

I didn't point out those details, at the time, since communism in Romania still existed. For some years following the collapse of the communist government, I felt the need to protect many people still remaining in the country.

Now seems like the time to put these details in proper order, and I have engaged someone to pen them for me. I charge each of you reading this not to hold anyone from the previous stories or writings to blame. As the saying goes "the names and places were changed to protect the innocent."

I am sure you can understand the need to protect those left behind. I pray that you enjoy the book and that God will use it in a mighty way.

Ilie Coroama

Therefore, since I myself have carefully investigated

everything from the beginning, it seemed good also to

me to write an orderly account for you...

Luke 1:3 NIV

TABLE
OF CONTENTS

SECTION THREE - The Promise of America

Section One
The Early Years

Before I formed you in the womb I knew you;
Before you were born I sanctified you;
I ordained you a prophet to the nations."
Then said I: "Ah, Lord God!
Behold, I cannot speak, for I am a youth."
Jeremiah 1:5-6 NKJV

RUN!

The blast of cannon fire rumbled across the forest floor shouting to all the inhabitants of the wood that it was time to flee. The missiles and bullets whistled through the air and mercilessly tore the leaves and branches from their moorings.

Clutching the child to her chest, the woman looked quickly for a new hiding place just as the thunder of horses' hooves began to be heard.

"Run, children. Run!" she urged, as she herded and pulled the other three children along, willing them to hurry.

The terrain of the forest floor was riddled with fallen trees and blasted limbs, and the children had to scurry over and around the fallen giants to keep up. The woman, mother to them all, was frantic now. She could hear the armor of the soldiers as guns slapped against saddles.

If found, they would probably be shot. Her oldest daughter might be taken for the pleasure of the invaders, and she feared her daughter's fate. Prayer was screaming through her mind now as the small band ran stumbling for some sort of cover.

As they rounded a thicket, there before them the ground opened up into a very large hole. One of the missiles had landed there tearing up the earth, forming a crater. Quickly, all of the children were shoved into the opening, and the woman lay over the top of them.

At that moment, her face became engraved in the mind of the small boy she had clutched so hard. His mother's face hovering above him, a picture of weariness and fear, smeared with dirt, and lips moving in a constant, silent prayer was an image that would last a lifetime.

The soldiers on horseback were upon them now; their thunderous advance making the ground quake. First, one horse jumped the hole and went on, then another, and then two more. They flew over so fast that they became a blur of hooves, saddles, and guns as the entire division moved over them, never seeing them lying beneath.

She waited and comforted her children, wanting to be sure the Russian division had, indeed, completely left the area. While she waited, she poured out thanks to her Father for once again providing the shelter they needed to survive. Her energy was restored, and she sang softly, crooning over her frightened babies while they lay hidden in the deep folds of the earth.

IN THE BEGINNING...

I was born in a leap year, on February 29, 1940, in the city of Vicov de Jos in the northern part of Romania. It is the area that borders the Ukrainian nation that was part of the former Soviet Union. This region, also known by the name Bucovina, has seen many wars. More than any other part of Romania, Bucovina has been trampled on by many wars and by the people who were fighting those wars. From this region came a Romanian called Steven the Great. Steven the Great ruled and reigned over Romania in the fifteenth century, from 1457 to 1504. The Turks were in a constant state of war, and Stephen the Great, on more than one occasion, joined forces with the neighboring kings to try to defeat the Turks. Before each battle, he promised that if he should win, he would build a church or monastery for God. History records that Steven the Great fought and won forty-seven battles. True to his word, he worked until his death in 1504, managing to complete forty-four monasteries and churches and began work on three more. All were built in the region of Moldova.

In 1944, Russia occupied Romania. Some of the monasteries built by Steven the Great are in what is now the Russian-occupied part of old Romania. The others, approximately thirty monasteries and churches, are on the Romanian side of Moldova. The most famous one of all is near Vicov de Jos, where I was born. It is located in a small town called Putna. Steven the Great is also buried there.

I was born into a Christian family. I had four brothers and three sisters. I was a twin, having a brother at birth. My twin brother died when I was seven months old, but God kept me alive and helped me grow during wartime and famine. Eight years before I was born, God did something miraculous in my mother's life. If it were not for this miracle, I would not have been born at all.

My mother had a very serious infection in her left breast. My father had sought help from doctors, but none could help. They sent her home to die in her own bed.

Mother was in terrible pain, and the family feared the worst. The family heard the testimony of a man of God who saw many healed after he prayed for them. By the time he arrived, mother was in the last phase of life, and our home was filled with relatives and neighbors. Some had come to say good-bye, as was the custom in that day, and others had come to see and hear the man of God.

When this man walked in, he went to her bed and asked if she could believe that Jesus Christ was the Savior and Healer. Mother confessed with her mouth that she believed. He witnessed and testified to her about many miracles that the Lord had done, and then he prayed for her. He laid his hands on her and anointed her with oil. At that moment, she sat upright in bed and began to cry out and pray. All of a sudden, she began to speak in another language! Many people became scared when she started talking in a foreign tongue. They had never seen nor heard such things before, and they were shaken. Suddenly, mother noticed that the flesh on the left side of her breast, the part that was infected, had come apart and fallen into her lap. Blood began to pour from the wound, and some of the women rushed forward to bandage the area. My mother was cleansed and fully healed. It was a true miracle because, from that moment on, she began to feel normal again. By that evening she was able to eat.

Everyone who witnessed this accepted Jesus in their hearts and began to worship. My mother's intimate experience with God began that day. She would talk to the Jewish people in the area and all the neighbors about what God had done. Even the doctors confessed that this was a miraculous work of God.

BIBLICAL AND LIFE APPLICATION

Everything that God does is based on patterns and principles laid out in His Word. The man who came to our house didn't start out by sharing God's miracles first with mother. Instead he asked if she had the faith to believe. Once she had professed with her mouth, he then shared stories to build her faith. Finally he laid hands on her and prayed for her healing.

This followed the pattern set in the story of the woman with the issue of blood and the synagogue ruler named Jairus. Jairus stated early on that Jesus could heal his daughter. The woman admitted to herself that she would be healed if she could touch Jesus' cloak. Her statement of faith was heard in the throne room of heaven. God witnessed her act of faith, and healing was given to her. When she was confronted, she had the courage to share her testimony willingly with Jesus, Jairus, and all who were within hearing distance. This strengthened Jairus for the news that his daughter was already dead. The woman's testimony of healing helped keep Jairus focused and steady in faith as Jesus continued on to his home to heal his daughter.

There are many stories about Jesus healing the sick. This story shows a good pattern to follow. So many times when Jesus was healing, his reputation had gone before him and building faith wasn't necessary. Today many people have trouble maintaining the faith of a child and need help enlarging their faith. Perhaps more healings would take place today if we simply asked for profession first, then bolster faith with stories, and finally pray for God's healing power.

As Jesus heard the word that was spoken, He said to the ruler of the synagogue, "Do not be afraid; only believe." Mark 5:36 NKJV

WARTIME

The Russian troops trampled the region of Romania where I grew up; I can still hear the sounds of the gunshots and cannon fire. The Russian army began its occupation in the spring of 1944, and we were forced to evacuate. My mother gathered what she owned, put it in a bag, and buried it in the forest. Just about everyone in Vicov de Jos hid their valuables in wooden crates, but not in the forest; they hid them farther south. A huge forest with hills and mountains all around was near our house, so we hid all the family things there.

Taking a cow, a sack of flour, and a big, goose-down comforter, we hid from the army in the forest. At night my mother would cover us with the comforter. I can still hear the sounds of the missiles, the guns, the cannon fire, and the bullets flying through the air.

One particular day, Mother was running with all the children, and she had me in her arms. She hid us all in a great hole. The soldiers that were on horseback jumped right over us and did not see us in that hole. This is imprinted in my memory. I cannot forget this because my mother was hovering over me and praying in that hole in the ground as the horses jumped over us and rode away.

Another day my sister, Elizabeth, was holding me in her arms when soldiers came and wanted to take her away. We were both crying, but because I was crying, the soldiers just left her alone.

Another memory is running and walking for days and days through the woods. As we neared a small village, we came upon one of our uncles. He was leaving with a wagon full of cheese, and he asked my mother if she wanted some for the journey. She asked if it was sweet or salty.

He replied, "Sweet."

So she accepted some of the sweet cheese. Just as we were leaving the wagon, a convoy of Russian soldiers came upon us with the intent of harming us. The soldiers were known to steal food and supplies, rape women, and destroy whatever was left. They were so mean. They attacked the wagon of cheese and trampled it under their feet. The food was too precious to be wasted, so Mother and I picked up the big pieces of cheese and tried to hide them. Then we all started eating as much of the small pieces as we could. When the soldiers saw us eating, they began to eat it too! They had been hungry but thought it was poisoned. After they had eaten, they let us go.

We walked on and passed through a village that was a ghost town. Everyone had fled in fear before the invading army. We traveled and walked for approximately two weeks. We walked to the northeast part of Romania. There was no forest there, just open plains. It was there that our cow died. We met other Christian brothers who had cows, and they shared milk with us. We stayed there for a few months. That area is now called Dorohoi.

From there we traveled to a small town called Dersca. It was on the way back towards our village. We hoped to get back to our town and unbury our clothing and other possessions that we had hidden. However, the Russians had put the border right through our town!

For the next few years, people would try to go back and unbury their things, but the Russians had put many landmines throughout the area. Many of our friends and relatives were killed as they tried to retrieve their belongings. Word traveled fast, and people began to not have the courage to go back to Vicov de Jos.

We dared to go no closer to the border than Dornesti; so we settled there. I grew up in the town of Dornesti, never knowing my father. He was like so many other men who never returned from defending Romania against the invading Russians. He had been recruited for emergency service and was assigned to the front lines of the war. He probably died somewhere in Russia.

BIBLICAL AND LIFE APPLICATION

Is any one of you in trouble? He should pray...
James 5:13 NIV

And pray in the Spirit on all occasions with all kinds of prayers and requests... Ephesians 6:18 NIV

Be joyful always; pray continually; give thanks in all circumstances, for this is God's will for you in Christ Jesus.
1 Thessalonians 5:16-18 NIV

As a small boy, the stories in this chapter were moments of fear and danger for me. I can't remember specifically praying at those exact moments, but then again, I was very young. My mother, however, never stopped praying, and her prayers covered us all. The image of her hovering over me, as we hid in that hole so long ago, has never left my mind. I often think about her faithfulness in the midst of crisis.

Her example of prayer stayed with me as I grew, and I learned from a very early age to rely upon the Lord.

Train up a child in the way he should go, and when he is old, he will not depart from it. Proverbs 22:6 NKJV

TRIALS COME EARLY

Shortly after settling in Dornesti, famine swept the region. There was a terrible drought; it didn't rain for over six months. Many, many animals died since there was no hay or food to feed them. I remember we received canned foods from America.

My mother would hold up the cans and say, "This is from America."

We would pray for America. Mother taught us to pray for other countries, and even as a boy, my heart was drawn to Japan, Israel, Austria, and America. Sometimes we would play a game called "jurzupe, jurzupe" in which we had to choose countries to be the captain over. I always chose these same four countries.

We were very poor, and my older brothers and sisters were forced to go to work for wealthier families just to feed themselves and survive. I was too young for this, so I was left with my mother. Once, during the famine, she left me alone and went to Constanta. Constanta is all the way on the other side of Romania, near the Black Sea, nearly seven hundred kilometers away. There was no food to buy locally, so everyone from the northern part of Bucovina Region would have to go a very long distance to buy a sack of flour.

I was around five or six years old when my mother left me to go buy flour. Mother was gone for several days. She left me with a little bit of corn flour in a bowl. I would put water on to boil, put some flour in the water, and eat it. One day the handle on the little pot broke. The mixture of flour and boiling water poured onto my legs badly burning me. I ran outside, jumped into a puddle of water in the street, and stayed there until a neighbor lady came and took me out.

Another time when I was six or seven, one of the older boys, Victor Cosian, took me with him to catch fish. My job was to watch his clothes to make sure no one stole them. Later, he wanted to cross the river, so he put me on his back and started across. The water got very deep, and I couldn't hold on. I lost my grip on him, slipped off his back, and sank deep into the water. I swallowed a lot of water and thought that it was over. I believed I was going to die in the river. Another boy on shore saw me and jumped in. He pulled me from the bottom of the river, which was about two meters deep. He pulled me out by the arm, put me stomach down on the shore, and the water miraculously drained out of me.

Since the time I was a very little boy, my mother taught me to pray and to not quit or give up, even when going through trials, tests, and hard times. Satan wanted to finish my life, but God had plans for me. He has never been too late to come and help me.

BIBLICAL AND LIFE APPLICATION

God has a plan for our lives. He knows everything that we have gone through, are going through, and will go through.

"For I know the plans I have for you," declares the Lord, *"plans to prosper you and not to harm you, plans to give you a hope and a future."* Jeremiah 29:11 NIV

The Bible also tells us, *"I will never leave you nor forsake you."* Hebrews 13:5b NKJV

We must walk in the assurance of those words daily and hourly. In doing so, we step into the faith that will take us through the tough times.

...we also glory in tribulations, knowing that tribulation produces perseverance; and perseverance, character; and character, hope. Romans 5:3-4 NKJV

Even when I would have bad dreams as a child, my mother would teach me to call out and plead the blood of Jesus. Any time I would have a bad experience, I would plead the blood of Jesus and be delivered. If I was sick, I would plead the blood of Jesus, and I would be healed. If I were going through hard, difficult trials, I would call upon the Lord and plead the blood of Jesus. When I was older and the police began to follow me, I had very great faith and called upon the blood of Jesus to deliver and protect me.

And they overcame him by the blood of the Lamb and by the word of their testimony... Revelations 12:11a NKJV

I was born in the little village of Oneaga in October 1945. Oneaga is near the town of Botosani in the region of Moldova in Botosani County. Famine struck the area shortly after I was born. The years of 1946 and 1947 were terrible years of hardship.

My father moved the whole family to Timisoara because of the famine. There were six children at that time, and I was the youngest. I had two brothers, Constantine and Mihai, but Mihai got sick when I was young and died. I do not know what he died from. I had three sisters, Paraschiza, Florica, and Aspazia.

My father was a farmer. When I was young, we had a small farm of about twenty or thirty acres. We had sheep and cows. Some of the produce and livestock was sold or used to barter for other things we needed, but most of what we grew and raised was used to feed ourselves.

When communism took over, our farm was taken from us. The government told us that if we combined our land and worked together as a team, we wouldn't have to work so hard. I don't know if anyone really believed them. I was little and don't remember what my father thought about the take over. The government collective now controlled all the land, what was grown, and how long and hard we worked. Each family was given an allowance of produce grown in exchange for their work.

The grain still had to be ground to make bread, so we would take our grain to the mill for grinding. We would have to give a portion of our allowance to pay for the service. We stored the corn, flour, and wheat in the attic. Potatoes were stored in a hole in the ground behind the house. We lived very simply.

I was born after the war with Russia. My father, Niculai, was taken as a prisoner of war and sent to Siberia in 1942. There he was forced into hard labor collecting bodies and putting them in mass graves for burial. He was a prisoner of the Russians for two years. He was let go in the fall of 1944 and dropped off near the border at the end of the war. He walked for twenty-one days to return home. Poorly clothed for this journey, he arrived with severe frostbite on his feet and legs.

Later, we moved to the region of Banat, the county of Timis, and lived in a small village called Berecsaul Mare. When I was eleven, an evangelist named Christu Barbu came to live in our village. He was Romanian, but his roots were Yugoslavian (Serbian). He started a home church in the area that was not registered with the government. Having a home church was illegal at this time but it was not yet under government scrutiny.

I was invited by friends to go visit, and I liked what I heard at the home church. I asked my family to join me. They also liked what was preached there, and we became good friends with the Barbu family. We would go to their house three times a week for prayer. We didn't receive any pressure from the Orthodox Church when we began attending the Barbu's home church. Since we had recently moved to the area, we hadn't been faithful goers to the Orthodox Church.

My mother instilled a knowledge of God in us from an early age, back when we were in the Moldova area, but I can't remember where this knowledge came from. She would pray with us even before we went to the home church. I remember Mother didn't like it when people used the word "Dracu" because it means "Satan." We lived in the Transylvania area, so the word was frequently used. To this day the image the word "Dracu" creates brings shivers to those who are older.

As much as I can remember, the only association my family had with the Orthodox Church came on holidays, like Easter. My mother would bake a loaf of bread, and we would take it to church to be sanctified, as was the Romanian custom.

I was baptized with my mother and sisters, but not with my father. The water baptism was held at a river called Bega. Although water baptism was illegal during this time, God protected us, and we were baptized without any problems. In accordance with an old Pentecostal tradition, you had to be 18 years old before you could be baptized. The people believed, at that time, that the act of baptism was, in essence, a contract with Jesus for your salvation. If you backslid, you would lose your salvation. They always wanted to make sure the children were old enough to understand and not backslide. When the elders found out I was only twelve, they didn't want to baptize me.

The elders had come to our area to ask questions of each person who wanted to be baptized to make sure they were ready. This is how they found out my age. When they told me I couldn't be baptized, I was very zealous.

I cried and begged, "Please allow me to take the baptism."

One old man, who had come with the elders, said, "We will give her the baptism because God can keep her close to Him."

I remember that old man to this day.

THE MIGHT SHEPHERD BOY

After I finished grade school, there were few options o̧
me, so I began to shepherd some sheep. This way I could ma̗
some money to help my mother and still have a little for myself
during the summer. I would collect money for every sheep I took
care of. I received two kilograms of flour and fifteen lei. During
the summer months, I took care of around three to four hundred
sheep. As a result, I gathered a lot of flour and made quite a bit of
money. Besides that, I had sheep of my own.

My older brother, Peter, and I learned how to milk the sheep
and make cheese. We learned how to care for different groups
of sheep. There were three different categories by age: older,
younger, and lambs. The older sheep were very productive,
producing wool and plenty of milk for cheese. From the younger
sheep, we harvested the wool. The lambs had to be raised
separately. We had to care for them in a certain way so that they
would become productive.

I grew up in a very legalistic, Pentecostal church in Dornesti.
My mother was a very committed Christian, and she had
revelations of God's grace and mercy. Mother always had a lot of
revelations, visions, and dreams. When I was about 12 years old, I
started seeking permission to be baptized in water. The Pentecostal
tradition said I had to wait until I was 18 years old. I had already
been baptized in the Holy Spirit, and I had different gifts operating
through me: visions, dreams, and the gift of prophecy. As time
went on, God began to use me through these gifts of prophecy and
visions that I would receive from the Lord. There were some older
brothers that would travel from church to church, and many times
they would take me with them.

From the time I was a teenager, the Lord had given me the gift
of reciting and composing poetry. I would be endowed with great
memory and could recite the Psalms. Sometimes the Holy Spirit
would give me extra words that would personalize the scriptures

...rson or group. At other times, I would recite from
...or Acts. God always gave me a song in my heart as I visited
the many area churches and recited poems. In spite of my youth,
God gave me great favor before people and churches, and many
doors opened allowing me to minister.

BIBLICAL AND LIFE APPLICATION

God uses the young. Throughout the Bible, He has placed
great responsibility on them. David was anointed to be king of
Israel.

*And Samuel said to Jesse, "Are all the young men here?"
Then he said, "There remains yet the youngest, and there he is,
keeping the sheep."* I Samuel 16:11a NKJV

Joseph was also very young when the Lord began to use him.

*...Joseph, being seventeen years old, was feeding the flock with
his brothers...* Genesis 37:2 NKJV

...Then he dreamed still another dream... Genesis 37:9a NKJV

Just like in the stories of these two men, great favor was given
to me at an early age. Doors, which should have remained shut to
someone so young, were open. I was bold in my faith, and God
used my circumstances, despite my age, for His purposes.

*Then Saul sent to Jesse saying, "Please let David stand before
me, for he has found favor in my sight."* 1 Samuel 16:22 NKJV

The Bible tells us to never despise youth. It may be our own or
the youth of someone near to us. God wants to use that youth for
His glory.

*Speak these things, exhort, and rebuke with all authority. Let
no one despise you [because of your youth].* Titus 2:15 NKJV

COMMUNISM TAKES HOLD

As time went on, the legally registered church was not able to operate free from government control. Manifesting spiritual gifts and speaking in tongues was not allowed. Many underground churches began to spring up.

This was the snare of communism—we will give you the freedom to have church, but we will restrict how you operate as a church. The pastors were given many rules. They weren't allowed to preach as the Spirit led. They weren't allowed to speak out against the government, the officials, or against the new regulations.

Pastors and believers alike were told, "You are not allowed to speak in tongues. You are not allowed to prophesy. You are not allowed to pray for the sick. You are not allowed to go from house to house and gather together."

Even traveling to visit relatives was strictly monitored and discouraged. This was a way to control the flow of information and spread of Christianity across Romania. If you abided by the rules and regulations, then you were trusted, and there were no problems. The underlying message was this—don't talk about Christ, don't share your gifts, and don't let anyone know your true beliefs. With time, it became very true and very real. The communists wouldn't allow you to share your faith. They said that if you shared your faith freely, you were spreading false propaganda.

This message was driven home when many older brothers and sisters in Christ, who did not obey the rules, were put in jail. Anyone who prayed in tongues, witnessed to another, or was heard praying for the sick was immediately persecuted. We never knew who was giving the government the names of violators. We soon learned not to trust anyone around us.

Inside me there was a desire that I believe was from God, and encouraged by my mother, to witness and tell other people about the Lord Jesus. When I was a small boy, I had watched a couple of my uncles work with a group to smuggle Bibles into Russia. I was inspired when I saw how great the need was in Russia for Bibles. I visited Russia and was able to attend some underground churches there. That is when God gave me the desire to someday send Bibles to Russia. At the age of 18, I began to come in contact with believers from the western part of Europe, from Austria and Germany. I met them through mutual contacts whom I had known since I was 15 years old. God arranged for this divine connection to happen. These men had lived in Siret, which was right on the border with Russia.

They began to tell me their secrets. They would show me how they operated and how they would send Bibles into Russia. They trained me and showed me how to do it. As time went on, it became a greater and greater desire and passion in my heart to learn more ways to secretly send Bibles into Russia. We had different strategies. We would train animals, particularly dogs and even sheep, to cross the border with Bibles tied to their chests. The animals would go across the border and mix with flocks that were owned by relatives, who used to live in Romania but were now on the other side of the border.

In the 1960's, I became involved with another underground network to smuggle Bibles into Russia. My brother, Peter, and I worked together hiding Bibles in the fields and in the forest. When it was safe, we would unbury them and secretly send them across the border into Russia.

From 1960 to 1962, we worked with these new brothers from Austria and Germany. Peter and I were just two of many people contacted by these people from the west. They offered additional training in how to send Bibles further into Russia. It was one of the most dangerous things I have ever done.

In 1970, we began to be trained by an underground network in evangelism and Bible smuggling. For two years, I was involved in a special, very intense, training program. An evangelical group from the west trained about thirty pastors and leaders for this. From them, I learned how to strategically go from place to place, how to place Bibles and other Christian materials in target locations, and disappear without being noticed. One of the most effective methods was to place Bibles in front of people's houses or in mailboxes. We would pass out New Testaments and sometimes even complete Bibles. Our training took two years to complete—two years of working with missionaries from England, Austria, and Germany; hiding in the mountains; and meeting in cabins. We changed locations daily to avoid being caught.

Over a period of a couple of years, our band of thirty pastors and leaders was able to plant over six million booklets, tracks, New Testaments, the Gospel of John, and complete Bibles all over Russia and Romania. Each of us was responsible for a different area. I was responsible for five counties near Suceava in Romania.

The secret police were really alarmed and began to publicly state that there were spies at work. As each of the original thirty trained leaders went forth, we each, in turn, trained two additional recruits per year in the art of Bible smuggling. In three years, we had been very successful. In the capitol city of Bucharest was the leader of us all, and still for safety reasons, he remains unnamed in this book. I was one who had direct contact with him, keeping him informed of the work in my area. I would tell him each month how many Bibles we planned to smuggle into Russia. The west, in turn, sent money for every Bible that was sent. In this way, we were able to support our families while doing the work of smuggling Bibles across the region.

The risk to my life was great. Every day, every contact made, every effort in the name of the Lord was a step of faith. I believed that He would protect me and shelter me from the eyes and grip of the secret police.

BIBLICAL AND LIFE APPLICATION

As we step out in faith to do the work that the Lord has placed on our hearts, we will, at some point, be met with opposition. It may only be a word here and there, or depending on where you live, you may face even more challenges. As long as we know from the beginning that no matter what Satan wants to do, he is already defeated, and we will prevail! His defeat came when Christ died on the cross and went into the depths of hell to take the keys from him.

The Bible is full of God's promises to protect us, as we are faithful to His call.

For the Lord your God moves about in your camp to protect you and to deliver your enemies to you. Your camp must be holy, so that he will not see among you anything indecent and turn away from you.   Deuteronomy 23:14 NIV

The Lord will protect him and preserve his life; he will bless him in the land and not surrender him to the desire of his foes. Psalm 41:2 NIV

"Because he loves me," says the Lord, "I will rescue him; I will protect him, for he acknowledges my name. He will call upon me, and I will answer him; I will be with him in trouble, I will deliver him and honor him. With long life will I satisfy him and show him my salvation." Psalm 91:14-15 NIV

Armed with God's word to protect me, I was able to boldly go out and spread God's word.

Now, Lord, consider their threats and enable your servants to speak your word with great boldness. Acts 4:29 NIV

Aurica's Journal

As life went on, I learned what it meant to be a good Christian. I loved to read my Bible and pray. Heavy persecution started in the mid to late 1960's. Pastors of area churches were told what to preach on, and they all used the same text on the same week. Controls came slowly, and we lost our freedoms a little at a time. The government would tell people that they were creating associations and teams, and putting new ideas into place. We were told if we worked as a team, life wouldn't be so hard. They were tightening the noose, but since it was gradual, people didn't notice until it was too late. Had we been able to see the big picture, an overall view, perhaps people would have been alarmed early on.

My parents decided to move back to Oneaga where they had a house, and I decided not to go with them. I was 17 years old. I moved to Timisoara, where I worked as a laborer in a candy factory. It was very unusual for a young girl to live alone. Most girls stayed with their families until they married, but I was ambitious. I rented a room from a Christian family there and settled into my life.

By this time, the communists wanted to control church programs, meetings, and services. We were only allowed to gather on Sundays, so we began meeting in secret at night. Every night there was a prayer meeting in someone's home. There were also spies planted everywhere, so you never really knew who was your friend. One night, I went to an apartment for a prayer meeting. They had two rooms. The back room had a sheet over the door. I was praying there with twenty to thirty other people in this little room when the police came in the front door. Our Bibles were spread all over the front room. While they were confiscating our Bibles, we all snuck out the back door. If we had been caught, we would have been fined approximately two thousand lei. It was very risky to go to prayer meetings. If you were caught at a meeting, you would be fined. If you couldn't pay the fine, you would be jailed. Many people were jailed because of this.

THE COMMUNIST GRIP TIGHTENS

The work we were doing was very dangerous, and the secret police and other communist party loyalists were everywhere. Many times I saw God confuse the police. He would blind them and cause them to not recognize me. Many times, I would be stopped, and they would ask me if I knew Coroama. God would always give me the right words to tell them; the words they needed to hear.

On one return trip from Bucharest, I had Bibles hidden in special compartments that had been built into my car. I had left Bucharest around four o'clock in the afternoon, intending to get home around three or four in the morning. I figured that most people (and the police) would be asleep at that time of the morning.

Driving through Romania you could always find people who wanted a ride. I had a habit of picking people up and witnessing to them about the Lord. I only picked up people during the day and early evening, never after seven or eight at night. As I was getting ready to leave Bucharest, I prayed with the brothers there, and a word was given that I needed to be careful. The devil was after me, but I was not to be afraid.

As I drove towards home, there was a section where the road forked. If I wasn't careful, I had a tendency to take the wrong fork in the road and head in the wrong direction. Sure enough, in the dark, I went the wrong direction. It only took me a couple of minutes to realize the error, and I started back. In a valley as I was returning to the main road, I saw a bride dressed in her bridal clothes flagging me down, desperate for a ride.

It was so strange to see a woman in the dark wearing bridal clothes that, at first, I was startled. I thought it was an evil spirit or, perhaps, someone wearing a mask. I began to pray, and God comforted me. I passed her and drove to the top of the next hill.

Then I turned around to go back and pick her up, but as I came back down the hill, God moved on my heart not to stop but to go on. I stopped immediately, turned around, and went back to the main road.

Soon there were bright lights in the rearview mirror coming up on me very fast. I could see by the shape of the headlights that it was the secret police. They caught up, passed me, and pulled in front of me. They stopped their car in front of mine, forcing me to stop. Two undercover policemen got out and came to my car.

Their first question was, "How could someone like you have a car?" That question was more for intimidation. The second question was, "Where are you coming from?"

I replied, "From Bucharest."

Their next question was, "Why are you lying?"

I said, "I'm not lying!"

They replied, "Yes, you are lying because your car was coming from Iasi."

I said, "Oh yes! Truly I wasn't paying attention, and I made a mistake. I went towards Iasi, realized I was going the wrong way, and I turned back."

They listened to my answer and demanded the following, "Who is in the car with you? Who is in the trunk?"

They looked in the trunk and found no one. Then they asked if I had seen anyone on the road. I replied that I had seen a bride, but I had been afraid to stop. Immediately they left and went the direction that they had come from.

In the Romanian Christian Orthodox traditional wedding, at midnight the bride would receive all her gifts, and usually, there would be a lot of money. According to tradition, the bride would go hide herself with the gifts and wait for the groom to seek and find her. I later heard from friends that this particular bride had a different idea. Instead of hiding, she had taken off with the money and had been looking for a ride. Two years later, they found her in Constanta by the Black Sea.

I would have been in so much trouble if I hadn't obeyed the prompting of the Holy Spirit. They would have found the girl, considered me an accomplice, and probably searched the car and found the hidden Bibles. I had been carrying so many Bibles that night that not all of them had fit in the secret compartments. Some were on the back seat under a blanket. I had set some food on top of the blanket. Even if they had never found the compartments, they would have found what was on the seats if they had searched. But the Lord kept me safe, and I arrived home very late—very tired, yet very safe.

BIBLICAL AND LIFE APPLICATION

History has shown that freedom is lost a little at a time. At one time, Romania was one of the wealthiest nations in the world. Ruled by a king, individual families owned land, profitable businesses, and their children were well–educated. As the grip of communism tightened, prices skyrocketed and the value of the lei plummeted. Romania lost everything; its wealth, private ownership, education, and *freedom*.

We must remain steadfast in our beliefs and fight for freedom as a whole, rather than allowing freedom to be chipped away one piece at a time. All too soon, you discover there is no freedom left at all.

If we don't know history and don't learn from history, then we are doomed to repeat it. Freedom is precious. Let's not take it for granted! It's our responsibility to be aware of what our leaders are doing. It's our responsibility to make up our own minds about policies, rather than allowing ourselves to be swayed by opinion or popularity of idea.

Only be careful, and watch yourselves closely so that you do not forget the things your eyes have seen or let them slip from your heart as long as you live. Teach them to your children and to their children after them. Deuteronomy 4:9 NIV

It's the same with Satan. He puts us in bondage little by little. No one ever wakes up and says, "Today I will have an affair or rob a bank." It's always preceded by many other small events or choices that lead down the path to that big moment. Sometimes, it's too late to regain your freedom, and you must wait in man's captivity. With God, it is never too late to make a change of heart. Any change of heart has to begin with you. God can and does arrange outside circumstances to draw one to Him, but the moment of decision rests squarely on the shoulders of each individual.

If you have never fully given your heart to the Lord, please, I encourage you to do so now before going any further in this book. The Lord has put us together for just this purpose, for just this time.

The Bible says, *"For God so loved the world [you] that He gave His only begotten Son, that whoever believes in Him should not perish but have everlasting life."* John 3:16 NKJV

Taking a moment to pray a simple prayer is all you need to set your feet on the path of eternal freedom. Acknowledge your life as a sinner and state that you need God to cleanse you and make you whole. Give your heart to Him, and He will do the rest.

"A GODLY WOMAN, WHO CAN BE FOUND..."

When I was around twenty, I started praying to be married. I was living in the Suceava area at the time but would travel all over the country preaching and smuggling Bibles.

In 1963, I was visiting Timisoara and met a woman named Aurica. We both felt it was the Lord's will for us to marry. We had words of God spoken to us as confirmation. I felt a calling to live in the Bucovina region and to continue the work in that area. The flow of Bibles from there had stagnated, and I felt that a major part of God's calling on my life was to send Bibles into Russia.

Just weeks before I was to be married, Aurica changed her mind. Many rumors and false accusations had begun to spring up about what I was doing. The Orthodox Church had labeled my work in the Lord's name as propaganda, and I was considered a spy by the government. Aurica listened to the murmuring instead of to God and refused to marry me.

I was shaken, not only emotionally because of her rejection, but my faith was shaken as well. I was sure I'd had God's approval beforehand, and I had been given words of confirmation from others. I spent a lot of time questioning what I had heard and felt. I returned to Bucovina alone and began the work there.

A couple of months later when I was free on vacation, I returned to Timisoara and met another young woman. After returning home, I began to correspond with the lady who is now my wife. At the time I didn't know her, but through our correspondence, I began to see her heart. It was a wonderful experience how the Lord answered both our prayers, and the way we met was a clear confirmation from God for us.

Isn't it just like God? Her name was also Aurica, and she was from a Christian family. Aurica was originally from the Bucovina area, a town called Botosani. She had moved with her family to Timisoara and had grown up there. After I felt I knew God's will, and I had the confirmations from the Lord that it was His will

31

for us to be married, I proposed to her. This time the Lord had led me to the right woman. When I told her that I felt it was God's will and calling for me to move back to the Bucovina area, Aurica was willing and agreed to move back with me. We were married in 1964.

BIBLICAL AND LIFE APPLICATION

We must always be careful to listen to the prompting of the Lord and be aware of his timing. I met two women, both named Aurica, and almost married the wrong one. I then spent time questioning if I had even heard God! Had I heard right? Aurica? I *had* heard correctly—I just had the timing wrong. With everything that God was going to have me do, it was crucial to have the right helpmate at my side. Each one of us needs the right helpmate. No one can know the extent of God's plans for their life. Each one of us must have a solid mate to stand firmly with us, and we, in turn, must be the solid helpmates that they need.

The Lord God said, "It is not good for man to be alone. I will make a helper suitable for him." Genesis 2:18 NIV

For many are called, but few are chosen. Matthew 22:14 NKJV

The first Aurica had listened to the gossip and lies of others rather than listening to God. Just like Jesus, I had been rejected by my hometown and accused of being a false prophet.

Praying for each other builds intimacy. Whether it is with someone you know and love, or someone you barely know. Prayer builds a bridge, a link, between you and the other person. In the case of Aurica and I, prayer was the foundation that God built our marriage on. If you aren't in the habit of praying for your spouse and family, begin today. You will see miraculous results.

And pray in the Spirit on all occasions with all kinds of prayers and requests. With this in mind, be alert and always keep on praying for all the saints. Ephesians 6:18 NIV

Aurica's Journal

I heard about a man named Ilie from the Bucovina region, Suceava County, who had come to visit Timisoara. It was very risky to even travel like that. It was very bold and courageous and went against all the laws. It was very risky and dangerous, and very few people would take such risks. I heard that he was on fire, zealous, and traveled all over the country. He was loved and appreciated by the people because of his zealousness.

I heard people saying, "He's coming. He's coming. Let's all go to see him. Brother Coroama is coming. Let's go there."

I went with my friend, Doina, to the home of a pastor who had a big church in the area. I saw Ilie there for the first time, but I didn't speak to him. Brother Coroama would minister and preach. He gave words of knowledge, and when he prayed for the sick they would be healed.

I heard others say, "Ilie is going to marry Aurica," a lady who lived in town. The wedding was scheduled for two or three weeks from then.

A few days later, I was coming home from working the night shift at the factory. It was about seven in the morning. I was just about to go into a store when I saw him coming down the street.

As he came near I said, "Hello Brother Ilie. Peace. How are you doing?" (The Romanian tradition is to greet each other with "Peace.")

I could see he was very sad, and I said, "I hear your wedding is coming in two weeks."

His response was "No. Everything got messed up."

He didn't tell me what had happened. I sensed his discouragement and tried to encourage him. We walked together and went to the open market where he bought some grapes to take to his mother.

After that, he returned to his home, but before he left I told him I would pray for him. We agreed to write, and eventually, we exchanged a couple of letters. I had no thoughts about marrying him. I just wanted to encourage him, and I kept my promise to pray for him.

The family I was living with kept telling me, "Oh, Brother Ilie is such a good man. He is a faithful man. I pray that God gives my daughter such a good man."

Everyone liked and appreciated him. At some point, Brother Ilie wrote to the family I was living with and inquired of me. They gave me the letter, so I wrote back to him.

After a few months, he returned to Timisoara, and we actually went on a date. He told me that he could feel my prayers, and we talked for a long time. We were married within two weeks in the biggest church in Timisoara. One of Ilie's friends was the pastor of the church, and he married us. We had no problems getting permission from the government to marry or for me to move with Ilie to Bucovina.

Thinking back, I didn't start out looking at Ilie as a possible husband. I had been praying, "Lord, give me a good and faithful man." I wasn't after fancy looks or money. I wanted a godly man. Ilie was a godly man, committed and zealous. I could see that God was using him. That is what attracted me to him. He was everything I had been praying for.

THE HAND TO
THE PLOW

My bride and I settled into our new life in Bucovina. We continued to send Bibles into Russia. Once in a while, I would travel into Russia to check how everything was going and to establish new connections with people in the region. As often as I went, I would pray that God would help me to personally carry Bibles in with me.

Our God is a creative God, and He gave me several different ways to carry Bibles into Russia. I used these methods in addition to the methods I learned in the underground training program. Every plan that He gave me was flawless, and none of those Bibles were ever discovered. Sometimes I would put Bibles in plastic bags and bake large round loaves of bread around them. I could put two Bibles in each loaf and carry five loaves of bread without the authorities getting suspicious. If I was stopped and questioned, I would just break off a corner of the bread, say it was my bread, and eat it. "We're a part of the bread" is a Romanian expression, and I would tell the officials this while eating.

Many times, the Holy Spirit would prompt me that a patrol was nearby, and I would stop and begin to eat some of the bread. When the patrol would find me taking a break and eating, they never put two and two together. Many times they would search me, sometimes strip search me, looking for smuggled items, but it never occurred to them to look in the bread. Once I reached my destination, I would break the bread open and distribute the Bibles.

Another God-given idea was to have some aluminum containers made, similar to large milk cans. I would wrap the Bibles in plastic and arrange them along the outer walls of the cans. Then, I would pour honey in and fill them to the top. When they would open the cans, all they could see was the honey. The authorities would close the containers back up and send me on my way. Depending on the size of the Bibles, I could smuggle up to twenty Bibles in each container.

However, the majority of the Bibles went into Russia in the hands of train locomotive engineers (mechanics). They were paid five hundred lei, which was a large sum of money at that time. For that amount, they would take in one bundle of fifty Bibles. For one thousand lei, they would carry one hundred Bibles.

The engineers would run the trains at night, and they would slow the trains down near curves. Someone would be waiting at those curves, and the engineers would just throw the Bibles out to them as they went by.

There was a special way that we communicated with them through codes. After they delivered the Bibles, they would return and let me know by greeting me with the word "Maranatha" and a page number from the Bible. This let me know how many Bibles made it into Russia and how much money they were to be paid. Many of the train engineers weren't Christian, but they weren't loyal communists either. They could be bought for the right amount of money. We supported many train engineers and their families through Bible smuggling.

BIBLICAL AND LIFE APPLICATION

Being prompted by the Holy Spirit isn't a blessing limited only to charismatic dynamos. It is a gift freely available to us all. As children of God, it is our duty to walk closely with the Lord and pursue the gifts of the Spirit. The Bible tells us that the Holy Spirit speaks in a quiet voice. Only those walking close enough to hear can take advantage of this prompting.

...And after the fire came a gentle whisper.
1 Kings 19:12b NIV

Determine in your heart today to draw closer to the Lord and ask for His gifts. Pursue Him as one pursues a lover. After all, He is the bridegroom. Train your spiritual ear to listen for His voice. Then—and this is the biggest challenge—obey!

Listen and hear my voice; pay attention and hear what I say.
Isaiah 28:23 NIV

Aurica's Journal

Life began with Ilie in a village called Dornesti. We had a little house near the hills and fields where the children used to go sledding. Ilie worked at a factory that made asphalt. We lived in this little house for five or six years. In that time, we had four children: Fivi, Daniel, Marianne, and Lidia. The house was one room with a wood-burning stove in the middle. The stove provided heat and was also where I cooked all of our meals. There was one cabinet where I stored all the clothes, and there were four beds. We had no running water and no electricity.

The house was always full of mud. There was no grass outside around the house, so the mud was always being tracked in through the door. I can't remember if the floor of that house was wood planks or dirt. I washed the clothes in the summer in the Suceava River. I would put the clothes in a wheelbarrow and go to the river to wash them. Then I would bring them back and hang them on the line outside to dry. In the winter, I washed them in a large container and then hung them up to dry on the line outside.

We eventually built a three-room house in Dornesti and moved into it. Two of the three rooms were finished with a wood floor. The third room remained unfinished.

By this time, Ilie was working as a shepherd; caring for the sheep of others, as well as our own herd of fifty. He had hired people to help care for the sheep. They would watch them and milk them, and Ilie would supervise the workers and make cheese from the milk. Then he would go and sell it at the market.

Once when Dan was five or six, he got lost among the sheep. A mean ram with big, round horns butted him in the stomach and knocked him to the ground. Ilie was so upset that the ram had hurt Dan. *(Aurica laughed at this memory!)*

During this time, Ilie was working with train engineers sending Bibles into Russia. Sometimes he would fill suitcases with Bibles, and sometimes we would bake loaves of bread and hide them in the bread. Someone from Bucharest would send us the Bibles to be distributed. There was a big hole dug in the center of the unfinished room, and we buried Bibles in plastic in the hole. Then Ilie covered it with dirt, and I piled clothes on top of that. Once, the police came to search the house, but they didn't find the Bibles we had buried.

CONSIDER IT ALL JOY...

One of the worst times I had was when one member of the Bible smuggling ring was captured and tortured. It was summertime, and I had a car that I used for smuggling. God had blessed me while I lived in Romania. I worked very hard. I had plenty and was always able to help other people. In addition to the car, I had a new home and new furniture. I had worked very hard as a young man and had saved a lot of money. My brother, Peter, and I still owned the sheep farm. I had a lot of sheep, cows, bulls, and pigs, which I would sell and make good money from them. I continued to make and sell thousands of kilograms of cheese each year. We lived well in Dornesti, and we had everything we needed. At that time very few people had a car, and I used mine for many smuggling operations.

I went on a summer trip back to Timisoara. The whole time I was traveling from place to place, I heard the Lord warning me that the enemy was following me. He was trying to harm me. I was to be strong and not to fear because the Lord would put the words in my mouth that I needed to speak.

My mother was waiting at my gate when I returned home. She said, "Oh my Lord! My precious son! Since the day you left, the secret police have been looking for you everywhere!"

The Lord hadn't allowed them to find me on my vacation with Aurica and our two children, Fivi and Daniel. They had searched the entire countryside, but we must have been one step ahead of them the whole trip.

It wasn't long before the secret police were back at my door, and they arrested me. They put me in their car and took me to Suceava to the secret police building. There they told me that they knew everything about me, that I was a criminal and a spy. They told me that my time had run out, and I would never be free again.

A few nights before this happened, I had a dream about one of the men who worked with me in the Bible smuggling ring. His name was John. I dreamed that John was beaten and tortured, and his face was all distorted because of it. Now as I waited in a room, sitting at a table, the door opened and I was face to face with John. He looked just as I had seen him in my dream. Of course, the room had been prepared and bugged with microphones.

John came over to the table and whispered, "Brother Ilie, these people know everything about us."

I immediately stood and said, "You are a brother to me? You know me?" (Through our training, I had learned to respond in this manner.)

John was shocked and laughter rolled out of him. He just kept laughing and laughing. As he continued, I backed over next to the wall. His laughter was uncontrollable, and he was yelling, "I have no oil and no brakes! I cannot stop!"

The police came in and asked, "What happened to him? Did you hit him?"

I said, "No. Take him from here. This man is not normal."

By now John's face had turned purple, and he was foaming at the mouth! Two policemen drug him from the room.

Another policeman asked me again, "What did you do to him? You hypnotized him. You have the devil in you."

And I responded, "How can you say you believe in the devil? I have Jesus in my heart. If you say you believe in the devil, then why don't you believe in Jesus?"

They hit me a few times and then brought John back into the room. Before bringing him back in, they had me stand in the corner with my face to the wall. When John came in and saw me standing in the corner, he fell right there on the policemen's feet laughing and cracking up. He couldn't control himself. He kept saying something about having no brake fluid.

This went on for two weeks. They kept trying to put us face to face, but John couldn't talk. I was severely beaten. My head was very swollen when they released me to go home.

My children asked, "Why is your head so big, Daddy?"

The secret police had warned me that if I told anyone that they had beaten me, they would kill me. Like everyone else, I had learned to never talk about the beatings and torture that I endured.

Later, I found out that while I was gone on vacation, John had given twenty Bibles to a tourist going to Russia. The tourist was a relative. They had made a plan to cross at a border that didn't have many control police. Unfortunately, they were stopped and strip-searched, and the Bibles were found. They were beaten terribly, and they confessed that they had gotten the Bibles from John. Immediately, John was arrested.

For eight hours they searched his house, and finally in the garden in the backyard, they found three thousand Bibles he had hidden there. That's why they had kept us imprisoned for so long, but when the laughter started, they couldn't get any information. They took him to doctor after doctor, and they all said he was insane.

Every time they brought him in, I would face the wall and pray. Eventually it got so bad that not only would John fall down laughing, but so would the police! I would just keep standing in the corner and praying. So they set us both free. If I had uttered one word, admitting what he said was true, they would have imprisoned us forever or executed us. I was working with over thirty people at the time, secretly smuggling Bibles into Russia. They suspected me very much, and they had found out from John that I was a ringleader. They had beaten John mercilessly, and he had confessed everything. Many people could have lost their lives had God not intervened on our behalf.

We had all received special training from the west, and when they couldn't get to me through John, they rounded up all the train engineers that ran the trains into Russia. The secret police told them that I had confessed everything, including giving the train engineers thousands of Bibles to take into Russia. At the same time, they were telling me that the train engineers had admitted to delivering thousands of Bibles into Russia for me.

The secret police asked if I wanted to meet the men face to face, and I said, "Yes."

They brought them in one by one and to each they asked, "Do you know this man?"

Each man, in turn, would reply, "I don't know him. I have never seen him. I don't know who he is." One by one they came, and one by one they gave the same answer.

It was a difficult time, full of trials, for us all. God saved all of us; not one person was put in prison. As part of the fear tactics, they had showed me documents, laws that stated that if three people together were doing this sort of activity it was considered an organized operation. They had the right to execute them on the spot. There had been over thirty people involved, but God had mercy on us all.

John never fully recovered his sanity because of the treatment of the secret police. He eventually died from the injuries he sustained.

The last time I successfully smuggled Bibles into Russia myself was in 1970. In the spring of 1972, I went to Russia again. Before going in, I sent Bibles to a church in the city of Cernauti. The church had about four hundred members, and they only had four or five Bibles. Ahead of my arrival, I sent a box of two hundred Bibles.

I went into Russia by train, and someone picked me up and drove me to the church on a motorcycle with a sidecar attached to it. It was very cold, nearly freezing, and I hunched down inside the sidecar to stay warm. We were driving without lights in the dark so that we would not be seen. Evidently we clipped someone on the leg, perhaps breaking it, while driving. My driver didn't know he had done this, and we went on to the underground church in Cernauti.

The church was packed when we arrived, and I made my way to the front of the church to preach. Just as I started, five secret police agents burst in yelling that everyone was under arrest and no one was to move. They came to me, and I was the first one arrested as a spy. They called for four vans to come and take the church leadership and me in for interrogation. The Bibles remained behind in a box by the doors, never to be discovered.

They took us all to the same building, and we were all severely whipped and beaten. Then we were clubbed with rubber clubs. They told me it was over and finished. They told me I would be executed. They told us all that we were dead men. They interrogated us in every imaginable way. They put us in a small, humid room with standing water on the floor. First fear came on me, but then I began to worship, pray, and sing in other tongues. Soon the others had joined me in song while the secret police watched us through small openings. They must have been thinking, "These people are insane. They are going crazy in there!"

The first two or three nights were the worst. Eventually we became used to it, and it was easier. They kept shuffling us around, not letting us stay in the same groups for long.

Sometimes they would add other criminals and even Russians to our group. The Russians would curse the authorities and try to get us to say bad things about them. The Russians would say that when they got out of that place, they were going to look for weapons or bombs, some way to kill the secret police.

I believe it was to try to get something out of us, but I would always say to them, "I am praying for these people. I have nothing against them. I pray for the Lord to save them." I would say, "I believe God really loves them, and that He has a plan to save their lives."

This went on for many, many days. It was a difficult time. They would feed us one piece of old, stale bread and one cup of tea with no sugar in it a day. My bed was made of wood slats with one blanket. It was very cold, dark, and smelly because the toilet was in the room too. It wasn't really a toilet. It was a hole in the ground. Once a week they would drain the water out and flush it. Once a day they turned a faucet on for us. The conditions were awful, and we all prayed continuously.

One night as I was praying, God said, "I will set you free. I will make a miracle."

Then after a few days of not being beaten, they took all the other church leaders out and left me there alone. I do not know what happened to them, or if they were ever released.

They left me alone and never added any new prisoners to my cell. I don't know how many more days I was there. One night, I don't know the time, but it had to be at least ten or eleven o'clock, I suddenly began to hear a lot of rattling and other strange noises. The locks were all being opened, and the cross bars were falling to the ground. I stood up, and in marched a general and a soldier.

The soldier held the door for the general who said, "Come this way."

I followed him, and we went outside. We went through two gates. Then another soldier took me all the way to the train station. There, another soldier, or perhaps a general, took over, but they never said a word. They just made signs. From where I was arrested to the train station was about a 20 minute walk. I hadn't been in a prison. It was only an interrogation point. They had beaten me and tried to get me to talk. It was so bad that I almost wanted to say, "Okay. Let me write down everything you want." That was how bad they had treated me.

I took the train to Dornesti, about a two-hour ride, and arrived home around four o'clock in the morning. I couldn't believe I was back at home. I kept thinking it was a dream or a vision. They had sent notice to the mayor, Galan, (he is still alive today and living in Dornesti) that I had killed someone with my car, and I would have to stay in prison and serve a life sentence.

But I was free. Praise the Lord! Later, I would remember one night while I was in prison, when God spoke to me and said, "One day you will be free. I will give you wings as eagles. You will be able to go to many nations and testify about My name. You will travel with a man that is right now in the highest place." I didn't understand that. I had thought, at the time, that I was going to die, and I was going to be with the Lord because He is in the highest place.

Fourteen years later, in 1986, I was visiting Kurt Waldheim, the president of Austria. There was a special meeting there with different leaders and heads of state. The president of Guatemala was there, as well as the president of Costa Rica. A man named Charles Duke had been invited to give his testimony about his walk on the moon. Charlie Duke stood up and said that it was fourteen years ago to the day that he had been walking on the moon. At that moment, I felt the Spirit of the Lord asking me, "Do you remember where you were fourteen years ago today?" I had been locked in that horrible cell in Russia.

(Brother Ilie broke into praise at this point saying, "The Lord set me free. The Lord is good! When the Lord sets you free, nobody can lock you up!")

BIBLICAL AND LIFE APPLICATION

Consider it pure joy, my brothers, whenever you face trials of many kinds, because you know that the testing of your faith develops perseverance. Perseverance must finish its work so that you may be mature and complete, not lacking anything.
James 1:2-4 NIV

It is hard to understand why we have to go through troubling times, but the Bible clearly tells us that it is for our own good. Without spiritual growth, we cannot take the place that God has designed for us.

The challenge comes in remaining focused on Him during the difficult times.

You will keep in perfect peace him whose mind is steadfast, because he trusts in you. Isaiah 26:3 NIV

The secret police brutalized my friend, John, and every time they wanted to bring us together for the purpose of exposing what we were doing, he would fall down laughing uncontrollably. While I have no specific biblical basis for this, how could this be anything less than a loving and merciful God? Only God could cause such an occurrence!

The jailhouse release has always reminded me of the miraculous release of Paul and Silas. In the middle of the night, there was sudden noise and commotion, and chains and bars were falling to the ground. Two men stood in front of me, and told me to go with them. While I have no way of knowing for sure that they were angels, I know what I believe, and I most certainly don't believe that the secret police just decided to let me go! They had already informed my family that I was in jail for the rest of my life. I was already labeled a spy. What possible reason was there for them to let me go? No. Truly this was a miracle of God!

About midnight Paul and Silas were praying and singing hymns to God, and the other prisoners were listening to them. Suddenly there was such a violent earthquake that the foundations of the prison were shaken. At once all the prison doors flew open, and everybody's chains came loose. Acts 16:25-26 NIV

And when Herod was about to bring him out, that night Peter was sleeping, bound with two chains between two soldiers; and the guards before the door were keeping the prison. Now behold, an angel of the Lord stood by him, and a light shone in the prison; and he struck Peter on the side and raised him up saying, "Arise quickly!" And his chains fell off his hands. ...When they were past the first and second guard posts, they came to the iron gate that leads to the city, which opened to them of its own accord; and they went out and went down one street, and immediately the angel departed from him. Acts 12:6-7 &10 NKJV

At some point they caught John. He was involved in Bible smuggling. He gave the police Ilie's name. For many months, they would arrest Ilie and interrogate him. They would beat him horribly for days and then send him home. Once they beat him so badly that his shoulder and arm wouldn't stop jerking. That time, they kept him for a couple of months, locked up in prison. I was so worried about him and feared for his safety! Sometimes they would release him in the middle of the night, and then follow him in a car to make sure he came home.

He wouldn't tell me everything that happened. He would tell me that they had threatened him saying, "If you tell her or anyone, we will come and cut your head off."

I was scared. I would cry and pray. We had five children at this point, but still I was begging him to go back to Timisoara. I thought he would be safer there, but Ilie refused to go.

We had a car, and soon the government decided to do an audit of our accounts to see how we could possibly afford to have a car. We only had enough money because Ilie was paid for every Bible he smuggled into Russia. Once the government realized that we shouldn't have been able to afford the car, Ilie would be in danger. One morning they came to the door and told Ilie to bring the car to the police station.

I had woken up that morning knowing that he had to leave. I had already gathered two pillows, a blanket, and sandwiches for him before the police arrived. I pushed all these things at him while saying, "Go. Go!" I was so relieved when he left. Instead of driving through town, he drove across the fields and escaped the police. Three times that day they came to the house asking for Ilie and demanding to know where the car was.

Each time I said, "I don't know. He left to bring you the car."

Later, I learned that God had been with him. A policeman, near the city of Brasov, had flagged Ilie down and ordered Ilie to drive him into town. He had a criminal to transport as well. Entering the town when the police were looking for him was a risk, but God provided him an escort—the policeman himself! And since God provides for all our needs, He also prompted the policeman to pay Ilie for a tank of gas!

Ilie stayed in Timisoara for a few days. During his stay, he sold the car and returned to Dornesti on the train. Almost immediately, the police stopped him.

They asked, "Where is the car?"

Ilie said, "I sold it to pay bills."

Eventually the police stopped asking about the car. We made a decision to sell our home, and in May, after school was out, we hired a car to drive us to Timisoara to live. Ilie got a job working in construction and did that for about a year.

Ilie started thinking seriously about leaving Romania completely at this time. We bought a very old house outside Timisoara in a village called Berecsaul Mare, and I started collecting materials to fix up the house. Terrible things began to happen to the men in the underground smuggling ring. Ilie seemed to think of nothing but the idea of escape night and day.

I knew God had placed the thought in his heart, but I confess I was terrified by the idea of it. So many of our family and friends had tried to escape, and we knew what had happened to each one. Many people that he prayed with had prophesied to him words of guidance and protection. I was terrified that Ilie would be killed. I was afraid for him. I was afraid for me, and I was afraid for our children—now six with one on the way.

After church one night, we went to someone's home, and a man there was praying for us. He had a word of knowledge for me.

"Why are you afraid, woman? Don't you know that I have always been with you, and that I am watching over you and your children? I have a great plan, a great work to work with you and your family. You have to be open and trust Me in a greater way. What God has begun, God will prepare and will use Ilie for a great work."

After that I was full of peace. I prayed, "Lord, let Your will be done. I trust You to take care of me and my children."

I went home, and the peace continued. I had a dream one night that Ilie was gone. The Lord spoke in the dream, "Everything is going to be fine. Don't worry. All things will work for your good."

DAVID IS CAPTURED

Our leader, David (name changed to protect him), had been found out. When the secret police captured him and searched his house, they found a lot of money, documents, and incriminating letters. They found pictures of me and all the other leaders, as well as documents and secret codes. The government announced throughout Romania that a gang of thirty criminals had been discovered, and our names were put in the paper. David was given five days to give them an inventory of everything he was in charge of at his job. Within those five days, a missionary, who was the head of the operation in Austria, came into Romania with a specially built car from England and smuggled David and his wife out in that car. I knew within a few days of his escape that he had gotten out of the country safely. The day after his escape, every one of us was arrested and interrogated.

They would say, "David has told us everything."

However, we had been specially trained not to reveal any information. For me it was easy because I knew David wasn't even in the country. We would be arrested and questioned, sometimes beaten for days or weeks, then released—only to be rearrested, beaten, and tortured again days later. This went on for six months. We were never interviewed together or held in the same facility, so we never knew for sure if someone was talking. It was two weeks before we actually got word that David had safely crossed the border into Austria. Once that news arrived, we were all calmer. Only one man named Cristian (name also changed) was held longer. He was from Bucharest and was close to David. He made some mistakes in his responses, so they kept him locked up for almost a year. As for the rest of us, they could not gain enough concrete evidence to prosecute us. Things calmed down, but they continued to follow us.

Some time after this, I was coming home on the train from Timisoara with two Bibles. As was their routine, the secret police followed me on the train. At this point the law stated that you could have one Bible in your house or one Bible on your person.

The secret police searched me and found two Bibles in my bag. I had come from a secret meeting in Timisoara where I had been given letters to hand deliver to local leaders. I wanted to bring a lot more Bibles back on that trip, but God had impressed upon me not to bring more than two. I also had about two thousand lei to use for sending other Bibles on to their destination.

I was arrested on the train, and instead of taking me off at Dornesti, the next stop, they took me on to Raduati. At Raduati, I was put in a cell in the basement. They left me there for a time and then took me upstairs to be interrogated. Before taking me upstairs, they strip-searched me. At that time I didn't have much on me except the money. They found some of the letters, which didn't have any details in them, so I wasn't alarmed at that point; however, I did have a very important letter from David in my shirt pocket.

The letter was thanking me for the great success I'd had in sending so many Bibles into Russia in the last few months. The letter would be very incriminating. In addition to the Bibles, he mentioned all of the phone books that I had sent to him, and he specified how many more phone books were needed from each region. I had been trained to read letters and then destroy them. However, I hadn't memorized the numbers yet, and now I was about to be caught with the letter. All kinds of thoughts raced through my mind. I could eat the letter or grab it and run, but none of these ideas seemed right.

As they began searching my clothes, the phone rang in the office, and I was left alone for a few moments with the clothes. The room had a wood-burning stove in it, and I quickly grabbed the letter and threw it into the fire. As the men reentered the room, there I was warming my hands over the stove. In a few seconds, the letter was burned, and my life was spared. Glory to God! This letter would have proven beyond any doubt that I was a spy.

About the same time, the secret police forced the president of the Pentecostal movement to send a list of all of our names and photos to every church in Romania. The list came with instructions to have nothing to do with us. We became despised and looked down upon. They called us the dangerous spies from the west.

BIBLICAL AND LIFE APPLICATION

The Bible is full of people who became despised after once having much favor. Saul despised David. Saul drove him from the palace, and David became a wanted man.

The very people Jesus came to free despised Him. The Bible tells us that His own town, the people who knew him best, received him not.

But first He must suffer many things and be rejected by this generation. Luke 17:25 NKJV

Being rejected by the very people who used to be so desperate for my company or for a word from me was hard. Each of us has, at one time or another, been on the receiving end of rejection. However, when you know who you are in Christ and what His plan is for your life, you aren't shaken to the core. It doesn't really matter what someone else thinks; it only matters what God thinks. Am I walking right? Am I sharing His Word with others? Am I acting in love towards those around me? Am I pursuing the dreams God has given me?

If you don't know who you are in Christ, or if you are unsure of His plans and purposes for your life, spend time in prayer pursuing this. You will note that I didn't just say to pray about it— I told you to pursue it. Pursuing requires more action from you.

Now devote your heart and soul to seeking the Lord your God. 1 Chronicles 22:19a NIV

GOD PREPARES

As time went on, I began to feel more and more that I would be moving soon. I began to train others to do my job, and eventually, they took over the operations. The last time I was actively involved in smuggling Bibles into Russia was in 1972.

In 1973, Aurica and I moved to the Timisoara area. I went ahead and was there about six months before Aurica arrived with the children. Timisoara is actually the name of the large city. However, the government refused to let us live within the city, so we settled in a small village near there called Berecsaul Mare.

At this time the government controlled all movement of the people, and you couldn't just move to another city like we do in the west. You had to have a reason to justify moving and then gain permission. I couldn't gain the needed permission to live and work in the city, so I worked construction in the Timisoara region. It was very hard, physical work. During this time, I was away from my family and only traveled home every other weekend. It was a difficult time.

I began to get revelations and prophecies that my time in Romania was drawing to an end. My work was done, and the doors were closing for me. As I traveled in Romania for work and met in houses for prayer meetings, there were many men of God who had different gifts of prophecy, and I would hear from them what God was showing them. Without them knowing what I was seeking, they would give me a confirmation that God was going to send me out of Romania. He would be with me, and I was not to worry or be afraid.

I submitted a request for a passport to Yugoslavia. I thought if I could get into that country, then I could slip more easily into Austria, which was free. Austria had a refugee camp, and if I could get there, I could ask for political asylum. However, when I made the request, I was told that I would never be granted a passport and to never request one again.

I knew that I was being followed throughout the area where

I was traveling and working, so I began to spend more time in prayer and fasting. In May 1974, I told Aurica what I was feeling and going through. I told her of the revelation and confirmation that the Lord had given me, and the overwhelming knowledge that I could no longer stay in Romania. At first she tried to encourage me not to leave because she was very afraid.

She kept saying, "Let's build a house." She would begin gathering materials for construction.

I would tell her, "My house isn't here. It is over the ocean."

I could see my house, through the eyes of faith. It wasn't in Romania. I knew it was in America. She never argued with me, but I knew she struggled with God as we experienced more and more difficulties in Romania. Aurica and I had six children at this point, and Aurica was pregnant with our seventh.

God used circumstances to show her what was happening. She realized and acknowledged that I needed to leave for my own safety. One day I finally told her that I felt like the day was coming very soon when I would be leaving. At that point, I had yet another confirmation that it was time for me to go, and that God was going to watch over me and protect me with His light and lead me by His vision. After hearing that word, I traveled a long distance, almost one hundred kilometers, to visit a woman of God who had the gift of prophecy and visions. She told me that she saw a light that would lead me out of Romania. This woman had never met me before.

Soon after that meeting, Aurica had a dream that God was going to protect me and go before me. This dream strengthened Aurica and did much to calm her fears.

In the meantime, I was looking at all possibilities for escape including swimming across the Danube River. It was very dangerous, and many people had lost their lives by drowning. Those who didn't drown were either spotted and shot while still in the water, or run over by patrol boats and cut to pieces by the boat's motor blades.

I trained so that I could swim under water for thirty to forty meters before having to catch a breath. People I could trust would time me with a watch. The Danube was a lot wider than this, so I would have to come up for air before swimming completely across. There was no way that I could see to safely leave the country. I was looking for the way to make it happen, trying to speed up God's plan, but there was no avenue open to me.

The year was now 1974, and it was a very hot summer. I worked construction during the day and went to secret prayer meetings at night. Every night I tried to attend a different meeting. There I would be encouraged, edified, and built up. During the day the enemy was right there, trying to discourage me and bring fear, but the Lord would always encourage me not to draw back or to fear. God promised that He had a great work to do in me and through me. God also told me to wait for the time that He had prepared. When the time was right, He would show me the way and open the door. I was not to try to find an avenue of escape. He was going to provide it.

During this time, God was building my patience. I didn't have much. Since receiving His word that He was going to provide the way, I was expecting it to happen immediately. But I waited on the Lord and continued to pray. I received new words. "Be perseverant and wait upon the Lord." It seemed as if all the circumstances around me were becoming more difficult. Doors seemed to be closing, and things became more and more cloudy. I was still trying to make things happen on my own, trying every possibility that I could come up with. At one point, I even gave money to a person who knew someone that promised to help me get a job in Germany, but nothing ever came of it.

Then God spoke to me again very clearly, "Wait. Be patient and wait."

But now something new was added—a date, October ninth. I fasted and prayed. The Lord just kept saying that the time was nigh and that I should seek Him. If I did, I would see deliverance and a miracle of the Lord.

I prayed, "Lord, how will this happen?"

The Lord spoke to me very clearly that I was not to worry or walk out of peace, but to rest in Him. At the right time, October ninth, the Lord would deliver me and two other people. At that time, I didn't know who the other two were. I prayed and waited, asking the Lord to reveal the identity of the two people, but God in His wisdom revealed nothing.

Two weeks before October ninth, we had a water baptism. It was illegal to have a baptism, but there were many people who had it on their hearts to be baptized. If I were caught, I could receive three years in prison for each person that was baptized.

We held the baptism at night in the river. The night of the service, there were so many people that came to our house. Some wanted to be baptized. Some were family or friends of those being baptized. We prayed together, and God gave me a word to share. The word was, "This night we will see a miracle, a marvelous, great work."

I was shocked and so was Aurica. As we went to the river, she was whispering to me, "What if there is no miracle. All these people are here. Where did that word come from?"

I said, "I don't know, but if the Lord says a miracle is going to take place, then He will make a miracle take place."

Midnight at the river was very dark. Another pastor and I waded out into the water, and then the people getting baptized waded in. It was so dark that we couldn't see each other. We all prayed together, and suddenly above us was a circle of light! It was so bright that it was like the noonday sun. The circle just hovered above us, and I could hear a choir of angels singing. I was the only one who heard the choir, but everyone saw the light.

The light lingered a few minutes above us. Then it began to lift, rising higher and higher, until we could not see it anymore with our eyes. We had stopped the service to see what would happen. It was a wonderful baptismal service. God protected us, and He did not allow the police to capture us there.

I left the next day and traveled to Bucovina to say good-bye to family and friends in anticipation of God's promise that I was leaving on October ninth. At that time, He gave me Psalm 37. I made a promise to God that if He would be with me, guide me, protect me, direct me, and watch over me that at the right time I would return to my country. I returned to Timisoara to await the day of His deliverance.

BIBLICAL AND LIFE APPLICATION

With God there is always a timing issue. Usually God moves at a slower pace than we want. We always want God to hurry up. Sometimes we take things into our own hands and just end up making matters worse. In my case, I kept looking for the way to make my escape happen on my own.   All the while knowing that nothing would happen until He wanted it too. We can waste an awful lot of time running around when we could and should be spending the time in prayer. The reality is that nothing is going to happen until we are spiritually ready. The only way we can speed up God's timing is to make sure we are fully ready.

Wait for the Lord; be strong and take heart and wait for the Lord. Psalm 27:14 NIV

Section Two
Winds Of Change

Also I heard the voice of the Lord, saying:
"Whom shall I send,
and who will go for us?"
Then I said, "Here am I! Send me."
Isaiah 6:8 NIV

ESCAPE!

The man in front of them was definitely agitated. Frantically whispering to them, he said, "Why are you here? Why tonight of all nights? The guards are everywhere! Leave this place now! Go. Go. Go!"

The three of them turned and bolted from the office as quickly as they had entered. They ran towards the back of the train yard. The night was very dark. The clouds covered the moon and not a speck of starlight shone. The shadows and the night mixed together, and they couldn't see where they were going. They could hear the alarm cry go up as they neared the freight cars that were being maneuvered into position for the next day's runs. They were moving on short tracks, and the trio began to dive and roll under the moving giants. The soldiers with their guns and dogs would not go under the cars, but around them, thus giving the fugitives a few seconds lead. The gravel scraped their hands as they dove and crawled down, under, and up again. Then free of the last freight car, they ran into a sunflower field at the edge of the yard.

The soldiers entered the field and were getting so close that the men could hear the thumping of the gun barrels on the soldier's backs and the panting of the soldier's dogs. There was a loud "whoosh," followed quickly by another and another. Then brilliant, red flares exploded illuminating the area above them. Deeper and deeper they ran into the field. The spiny hairs on the plants seemed to clutch at the men like little demons trying to capture them.

Strangely, Ilie wasn't afraid even though a part of him knew he should be terrified. He drew strength from the scriptures. Even now the verse, "I will never leave you nor forsake you," was thundering in his head as loudly as his heart was pounding in his chest.

He didn't know what Pete and Paul were thinking, or if they were too terrified to think. Farther into the field they ran, into the open again, and then down into the next field. This one was a cornfield. It was a momentary relief to be free of the sharp, spiny needles. The feeling was quickly replaced by the razor edges of the corn blades. The corn sliced at them as they pushed ever forward into the field. Ilie became aware of the others around him, as they began to slow their run. The heavens suddenly opened without warning, and a heavy rain began to fall. The dogs would have a hard time now, as the men's scent would be washed away. The shouts of the soldiers seemed to grow fainter with each passing minute.

The three of them huddled there, sucking in huge gulps of air and easing their shaking knees into the cold mud of the field. Shouts of praise to God for divine deliverance were bursting in their throats, but they dared not utter a word. They offered silent thanks and continued to hide, waiting for God to reveal the next step on their road to freedom.

COUNTING THE COST

Before I left, Aurica and I prayed without stopping. The Bible verse about praying without ceasing began to take on new meaning for me. Every day we would hear stories of people who had tried to escape. Most would be caught before reaching the borders. By this time, most of the borders had been set up with different systems such as trigger alarms, border guards armed with machine guns, flares, and dogs. Often, people would trip a wire causing flares or alarms to go off. Many people would be shot right there at the border rather than being brought back for interrogation.

Others would try to swim the Danube. Many drowned or were shot when they came up for air. Some would be run over by police boats. In Yugoslavia there is a cemetery called the Cemetery of the Unknown. In it are hundreds of Romanians that the Serbian people found washed up on the shores.

People believed that the borders were so heavily guarded that there was no way to escape. Those who made it over the border to the refugee camps would have to deal with spies. These spies had been planted to discourage people from going to America and to encourage them to return to Romania. The spies would tell them they had been to America and had lived there for many years. They would say that America was a terrible place, that there was no work, and that the land was full of criminals that would attack you as you walked down the street. Many people believed the lies, would be discouraged, and return to their homes in Romania.

Once back home, they would be a discouragement to those around them to not even bother trying to leave. Many of these people would lose their minds or live horrible, bitter lives because of their decision to give up on their dreams of freedom.

One of my nephews tried to escape two or three times before he finally made it. Each time he was caught, they would beat him severely. They would kick him in the head with their boots and allow the dogs to bite him. He had scars all over his head, back, and body. Another friend was so badly beaten that, to this day, he has health problems.

Many people would be captured, tortured, and die from the treatment. Many others would lose their minds, and still others were handicapped for the rest of their lives. Satan wove these stories and images through our minds daily. We were in a constant state of battle to control our thoughts and keep our eyes focused on God and His promise to deliver us safely.

BIBLICAL AND LIFE APPLICATION

Fear is a bondage of Satan. The Bible tells us that fear is not from God.

For our struggle is not against flesh and blood, but against the rulers, against the authorities, against the powers of this dark world and against the spiritual forces of evil in the heavenly realms. Ephesians 6:12 NIV

Our minds are a constant battleground that we must work to keep open so that we can hear the Holy Spirit. Every act of sin begins in the mind.

Finally, brothers, whatever is true, whatever is noble, whatever is right, whatever is pure, whatever is lovely, whatever is admirable—if anything is excellent or praiseworthy—think about such things. Philippians 4:8 NIV

Do not conform any longer to the pattern of this world, but be transformed by the renewing of your mind. Then you will be able to test and approve what God's will is—his good, pleasing and perfect will. Romans 12:2 NIV

Finally the Bible tells us, *"Where there is no vision, the people perish."* Proverbs 29:18a KJV

We must constantly be checking in to see if there is any new revelation to add to the plan God has already revealed to us. Without fresh vision, we become stagnant. While we may still be productive and bear fruit, we are not producing as much or in the area where it is needed the most. Eventually we can burn out, as the flame of vision grows too dim.

The people who escaped Romania had a fresh vision. Those who returned lost their vision, which led to many miserable lives and years lost or completely wasted. We must constantly guard, grow, and nurture every vision that God gives us. Sometimes we may have to wait for the completion of that vision. It will happen in His timing, but it will eventually come.

...Write the vision and make it plain on tablets, that he may run who reads it. For the vision is yet for an appointed time; but at the end it will speak, and it will not lie. Though it tarries, wait for it; because it will surely come. It will not tarry. Habakkuk 2:2-3 NKJV

WALK IN THE LIGHT

October ninth was all I could think about. A week before that date, I took time off from work and spent most of it in prayer and fasting. I was still asking God how it would happen and looking for the way, but the Lord just kept saying, "Wait for the time. Wait because the right moment is coming. When the right moment comes, I will show you clearly."

October ninth was a Wednesday. That morning I woke with great joy in my soul. I felt as if I had a great light shining in and around me.

God spoke to me, "This is the day. This is the day of deliverance."

A few days before, God had given me a list of items to pack in a bag: a small Bible, a flashlight, two rolls of summer salami, a plastic bottle full of water, and a little bottle of vitamin C tablets. The Lord had also given me instructions on how the food and vitamins were to be dispersed. The bag sat at the door waiting for the right moment that God had promised me for so many months now.

In the afternoon, two men named Pete and Paul came to the house. I had met Paul before. Paul was about to be put in prison. He worked in a warehouse near the train station and had hidden two brothers between two pallets of feathers. He had loaded the pallets and sealed the train car. Unfortunately, the brothers heard German being spoken at one of the train stops and had erroneously assumed that the train was in free Germany. They had been captured, sent back to Romania, and imprisoned for five years. I heard that they were so badly beaten that they were not normal afterwards.

Paul had been an accomplice in this, and the authorities had given him a few days to make an inventory of his warehouse before they arrested him. God had spoken to him to come to my house that day.

Pete, Paul, and my family prayed together. Once again God

clearly said to me, "This is the day when you have to leave your country, your house, and your family. Your steps and your life will be guided by My light and My power."

As afternoon turned into evening, we sat down to our last meal together that Aurica prepared for us all. We ate, and again we prayed. Then I turned and kissed my wife. I kissed my children. The hardest moment was when I had to separate myself, knowing that I was finally leaving.

My mind was overwhelmed with negative thoughts. Fear was circling me and filling me with images of being shot and killed, and the thought of never seeing my family again. It seemed like the nightmares that I had battled for so many months now were actually happening, but I was awake. The difference was that with the nightmares I would wake up and pray. Then I would receive joy and a reprieve from the mental and spiritual battle. Now there was no rest. The onslaught was constant. I kept praying silently, calling upon the blood of Jesus, while I kissed my family good-bye. We prayed one last time together, and the Lord spoke to us to go out. This would be our first step of faith.

I opened the door and stepped out into the darkness. There in front of me in the road was a whitish-blue, neon-looking pillar of light! It was hovering off the ground approximately three feet and rose straight up in the air approximately ten feet. It glowed but gave no heat.

In my spirit I heard a voice say, "Follow the light. Look neither to the right, nor to the left, nor behind, but follow the light." The vision of the light would appear and disappear periodically. Many times I could see the light with my literal eyes. Sometimes I saw it through the eyes of faith. Sometimes a very bright, shiny star would appear. Paul also saw the vision, but Pete never did.

We started to go in the direction of the nearest train station, walking for nearly forty-five minutes to reach it. There we slipped onto a train that was going to Jimbolia, which was about an hour away by train.

Jimbolia was a dangerous place. As soon as the trains would arrive in Jimbolia, three guards would search every person. It was the last border town before entering Hungary. Every train exit would have guards stationed at it so that no one could leave the train without being searched. There were three different guard units represented there, and you had to pass through each one. First were the soldiers, second the police, and third were security guards or the secret police. The secret police always dressed in civilian clothing, so you never knew if a fellow passenger would turn out to be your enemy.

Everyone living in a border town had an identity card and a photo ID. The identity card proved which border town you lived in. If you couldn't prove you lived in the town you wanted to enter, then you couldn't enter without special permission. Without proof, you were automatically suspected and arrested. If you said you were there to visit a friend, you had to give your friend's name. They would send a soldier with you to that person's house. Your friend would have to fill out a request and guarantee that he would be responsible for you the entire time you were visiting.

We left the train and followed the pillar of light. The different patrol groups were stopping all the people in front of us. They were being questioned and searched, but none of the patrol groups stopped us. We just walked right through all the people and passed all the guard units! We walked to the other end of the train station and weren't stopped even once.

At the back of the train station, there was an office where a Christian brother worked. He was responsible for transit. He actually lived in Carpenis, but had permission to work in Jimbolia. We wanted to ask him if there were any trains leaving Romania.

When he saw me and realized what we were doing, he grabbed his head with his hands and came near me whispering, "How were you able to get to this place? This is the worst night possible for you to be here. The strictest control guards are here tonight. Please, I beg you, leave immediately. I do not know you, and you do not know me!"

Then just before we turned to go, he whispered, "The train on track five is headed to the west!"

We left the office and headed towards the back of the station where it was dark, looking for a place to hide. It was where the freight cars were kept. At some point we realized that we were being followed, and they were gaining on us. We started running and crawling under the freight cars that were moving into position to be linked up. The person who was following us didn't have the courage to crawl under the cars, so he ran around the units. We got through the trains and ran into a sunflower field at the edge of the station. I could see the different lights and signal wires that would send the alarm out to the rest of the soldiers. The freight area of the station was kept dark on purpose so that escapees wouldn't be able to see the trip wires. These trip wires would go off and signal the border patrols that people were in the area, and here we were running through the middle of it!

We could see the flares and other signals being shot into the air around us. Soldiers on the border would shoot red and white flares. This signaled others that someone was trying to escape. We stayed in the sunflower field, and later in a cornfield, hiding, waiting, and praying. The fields where we hid were right between two border patrol towers. We could see the soldiers from where we were hiding.

Within minutes, God sent a tremendous, great rain that quickly swept across the area. After the rain began to subside a bit, the light began to lead us back in the direction of the train station. We followed, crawling under some of the freight cars, until the light suddenly stopped at one of them. There was no way to count the train tracks in the dark. We checked the car the light had stopped at. The door to the car was barely open. A skinny person could squeeze through the opening, and we were all pretty skinny at the time.

We squeezed through to find the inside of the car full of mats, like reed mats. They were bound and stacked on top of each other. We crawled, maybe one meter in depth, beneath them. We just laid there and waited. As time went on, we could hear the noise of people walking around the freight car and whispering to each other. Great fear came upon us, but God spoke to me, "Don't be afraid. My hand is upon you."

BIBLICAL AND LIFE APPLICATION

During this segment of recording, Brother Ilie stated the following:

Praise the Lord. It's wonderful to praise God and to walk in His excellence. Two things are very important for us to understand and to obey.

1) *We should always realize that we are to obey God in everything He tells us.*

2) *We need to know and understand that if we are in His will, He wants to do wonderful things but in His time and in the right way, the best way. We need to understand what His will is and obey it.*

As I humbled myself before God, He gave me many revelations and visions. The pillar of light is just one example of receiving God's vision. The pillar of light was not with us constantly. It would appear and disappear. It came at times of extreme fear and need as we prayed for direction and wisdom. Sometimes we never saw the pillar of light, but instead heard the audible voice of the Holy Spirit speaking to us, meek and very gentle.

Each of us on a daily basis needs the guidance of the Holy Spirit. We'd like to always have a pillar of light to follow or hear the audible voice of the Lord. The reality of daily living is that God needs us to be the one that slows down, waits, and listens. I have never seen the pillar of light at any other time in my life. God doesn't have to communicate through signs and wonders for me to follow Him or to acknowledge His presence.

The night Ilie escaped was a night of peace. During the day, two men arrived at our house. I had never met them, but Ilie knew one of them. I made something to eat for them and fed all the children. Then we all prayed together, and I watched Ilie and the other men slip out into the night.

That was the last time I heard from Ilie for a long time. My days were filled with survival, taking care of the children and finding enough food to keep them fed. I had to haul water and wash the clothes. I had to gather wood for the fire to cook and heat our house.

It was so hard to maintain a positive attitude around the children, to not let them see my fear and emotions. The children always seemed able to pick up on what I was thinking and feeling, just by searching my face, and I had to work to keep my fears from infecting them.

I was several months pregnant at this time, and I pushed myself physically to care for the children and the rest of the household chores. I struggled with a nagging cough and always seemed on the edge of being completely worn out.

Throughout each day, I was in constant prayer for Ilie, the children, our unborn baby, and myself. I battled doubt, as images of my dear Ilie captured or dying would flash through my mind.

After about a month, a policeman came to the gate and asked, "Where is your husband? When did he leave?" My stomach seemed to flip and drop as I looked into his leering face.

TRAPPED!

In my spirit, I could still hear the Lord's voice saying, "Don't be afraid." On the outside of the car, I could hear the voices of the enemy circling and trying to stir up fear within us. We were all praying, and as we prayed God gave us the power to stand firm. Suddenly, someone was trying to get the door open! He couldn't get it open, so others came to help. It was stuck or perhaps the people were better fed than us and couldn't squeeze through the opening. Someone managed to pry the door open further, and a soldier with a dog climbed into the train car. The soldier started walking around on top of the mats, and the dog was jumping around and sniffing while we lay just inches beneath them.

We lay frozen underneath them, not daring to breathe, praying that we would not be found. We were waiting, second by second, to see what was going to happen next. A million thoughts raced through my mind at once. What would my family do if I were caught? What if I were executed? How would they survive? Memories came crashing through all at once—my mother's face, my wife's voice, the laughter of my children. The memories assaulted my mind in a single moment. My heart was beating so fast that it seemed close to stopping. Fear and panic were shrieking at me, circling me like devouring lions. Yet over all, there was an unexplainable peace despite the situation. Suddenly, I heard the soldier order the dog out of the train car. Before the soldier left the car, he took a sharp object, possibly the blade on his gun, and stabbed it through the mats in several places. One of the stabs came within a hair's breath of my leg. It was so close that I could feel the coldness of the steel near my skin. It was a very, very scary moment. I know my heart nearly stopped beating for those few seconds.

After a few minutes, I felt him climb off the mats and heard him jump out of the car. The door was forced closed and locked. We heard them walking away. Suddenly, we could all start breathing again. Of course, we never stopped praying and thanking God for His protection. We stayed there, under the mats, for the rest of the evening, and around midnight the train started moving. We didn't know where we were going.

All we knew was that we felt the presence of the Lord and heard His voice saying, "Don't be afraid. I am with you. I am with you. I am with you. Don't be afraid. I am in charge, and I am the engineer of this train. I am the driver. Wherever I want you to go is where this train will end up."

So we stayed there, lying under the mats, rocking to the rhythm of the rolling train. There was nothing for us to do, and for many days we rode in the boxcar. At night when it would get very cold, we would burrow deeper, letting the mats act as a blanket for us. During the day as the sun would heat the car, we would work our way back to the surface. We were always ready to hide again under the mats. Many times the train would move for hours and hours, non-stop. Then it would make a sudden stop, staying still for sometimes a whole night or half a day. We had no clue where we were or why we had stopped. After a week, waiting became difficult. Every day seemed very long, and the nights even longer.

Pete was starting to show the strain. His was a constant stream of incessant chatter. He had to get out of the train car. He couldn't stand it any longer. Day after day, this was what he would say. I would pray for him, and we would pray together.

The Lord would speak very clearly to us, "You have to wait and stay here until the right time that I will determine. I will show you when you need to get out of this train car. I will speak to you. Rest. Wait and rest."

Waiting was very difficult. The only way time seemed to pass quickly was when we were praying or reading our Bibles. Unfortunately, there were only a few slivers of light streaming in through cracks in the train car. There were no windows, and the soldiers had been able to close the door tightly and seal it. We spent our time in prayer and read our Bibles whenever there was enough light to read by. We found that those were very precious times, and the hours passed very quickly.

So many, many days passed while we waited for the Lord to

78

speak to us. The air was dank and close by now. Each day we sipped a little water and ate a bit of one of the salami rolls during our wait. We took one vitamin C tablet daily, letting it dissolve in one mouthful of water. This was in obedience to the instructions God had given me before we had left on our journey. As each day passed, a new language was heard. Hungarian at first, then days later Yugoslavian, and finally, what sounded like Italian. We could hear the announcements over the loud speakers, and people talking as they passed the car.

So we waited. We desired with a passion to get out of the boxcar. We had been locked in on October ninth, and it was now the twenty-sixth. We desperately needed water. Finally, the Lord spoke and told us that we would need to get out of the car at five o'clock the next morning. Just exactly as the Lord had said, at five o'clock the next morning, the train stopped! There was a metal window that had been closed for the trip and locked in place. We all pushed with our legs and bent the metal making a crack big enough for us to slide through. One by one, we helped each other out of the car and slid to the ground. We held each other. All of us were too weak to stand. We were also out of balance from being confined in a cramped area on the train for so long. We started slowly walking and within minutes came upon a water pump. We pumped up the water and drank. We washed our faces and hands. Then we drank more, filling our empty stomachs with water.

We started walking again, but we had no idea where we were. We saw that we were at a train station, but it was still dark. Morning hadn't yet dawned. Soon we could make out in the darkness a sign that read "Venice Train Station." We rejoiced greatly. We were finally free!

BIBLICAL AND LIFE APPLICATION

Waiting on the Lord is hard—very hard. We felt the strain of waiting, not only mentally and spiritually, but also physically. I think the physical aspect is the most interesting. Depending on the circumstance that you are in, waiting on the Lord can be physically demanding. Sometimes it is painful and uncomfortable, but the blessings come when we are obedient to wait. For the three of us, not waiting would have meant our lives. We may not face life or death on a daily basis, but we must still learn to wait on God. If we don't, we can miss what God has for us by rushing His timing.

Wait for the Lord; be strong and take heart and wait for the Lord. Psalm 27:14 NIV

And so after waiting patiently, Abraham received what was promised. Hebrews 6:15 NIV

THE SWEET TASTE OF FREEDOM

So there we were with our first taste of freedom! Venice, Italy, was the first free city and the first free country we were in. Our rejoicing was beyond measure! During the time on the train, we had eaten only one of the salami rolls, and we had a whole one left. We went and sold the salami to a little store. With that money, we were able to buy some postcards to send to our families to let them know we were alive and well. Our hair had gotten long, and our beards were thick and hairy. We had to get haircuts and shaves. From there we went to the police.

When we arrived at the police station, we told them that we were from Romania and that God had helped us and delivered us. The police took us into their office. They were very surprised that three Romanian men had escaped. They took our fingerprints and wrote down our interviews. We had decided in advance to change some details of our story, knowing that our Christian brother at the train station could be in danger. Also we had broken the window escaping from the boxcar, and we feared retribution for that. Since we knew we would be questioned separately, we needed to make sure our stories matched. We told them our agreed upon story. We told them we had walked across the border and snuck onto a train in Yugoslavia, not knowing in what direction the train would take us.

They were very nice to us. They brought us food to eat while they talked with us. The police kept us there until evening, and then they took us to the train station and boarded the train with us. We got scared because the train schedule said it was going to Yugoslavia. Pete was especially scared, but the train stopped at a refugee camp in the town of Triest before the Yugoslavian border.

When we arrived in Triest, it was night again. We were met at the station by another group of policemen. They put us in a closed van and wouldn't explain anything to us. We were afraid, but there was nothing we could do except pray. They drove us through a forest and along mountain roads. We arrived at our destination in the middle of the night. We were handed an emergency kit with some essentials so that we could wash and shave, and toothbrushes so that we could brush our teeth. It was only then that we realized we were in a good place.

BIBLICAL AND LIFE APPLICATION

As the police boarded us onto a train headed towards Yugoslavia, we were operating on a level of blind trust that the Italian police were, in fact, different than the police we had left behind. We could not afford to compare the police in Italy to the police in Romania. To do so would have laced our reactions with fear. We might have tried to maintain control of the situation rather than trusting the police to work in our best interests. In the same way, we must have blind faith and trust that God is operating in our best interests at all times. We must leave the circumstances of our lives in His capable hands rather than continually trying to be in control.

Trust in the Lord with all your heart and lean not on your own understanding; in all your ways acknowledge him, and he will make your paths straight. Proverbs 3:5-6 NIV

Blessed is the man who makes the Lord his trust, who does not look to the proud, to those who turn aside to false gods. Psalm 40:4 NKJV

The policeman asked again, "Where is your husband? When did he leave?"

There was evil delight in his eyes as he relished my situation, taunting me again and again. I recognized that the taunting was not coming from the man but was, in fact, from Satan. I stood my ground and refused to let fear wash over me. I told him that Ilie had left for work weeks before and had never returned.

The policeman asked again, "Where did he go?" Then he said, "He left you!"

He showed me a postcard. He was reveling in the fact that he could bring me what he perceived to be bad news. I took the card and read it. My heart leapt for joy! The card said that he had arrived safely and had been led by a powerful light.

The policeman said, "What light is this? It is the devil's light! He left you and the kids. He is a criminal. If you want to divorce him, you can do it immediately!" The devil continued to taunt me, through the policeman, celebrating that he had destroyed a family.

But I said, "No, I can't. He is the father of my children."

I continued to stand my ground, shaking with an emotion I hadn't felt in a long time—joy. Eventually he tired of the game and left me with the postcard. I rejoiced greatly after the policeman left. God had taken care of my Ilie and had led him to safety.

After that, the police came often, and once I wasn't home when they came. They started questioning Fivi as to where her father was. When I returned home, I found all my children hiding in the attic, crying. The children were so frightened! I was so angry with the police for bothering the children that I marched straight down to the police office and ordered them to never bother my children again. I was very strong (stern) with them.

No one ever went to the police building voluntarily, and I had marched in and told *them* what to do! They weren't used to it, and God was with me. I suppose I could have been in big trouble, but as it was, the police never bothered the children again. In fact, the police were now afraid to bother me. They were afraid I would somehow get word to Ilie that I was being harassed and that he would let someone know what was going on inside the country.

Iliuta was born in February while Ilie was out of the country. I was raising four pigs for the government, and I had two calves to care for. I was working very hard to keep everything going, and winter came early in October that year. I continued to be sick with a very bad cough, then I gave birth to Iliuta. I was worn out. I had an X-ray done after Iliuta was born, and they found a black spot on my lung. I was told to get treatments, but by then the cough was gone. Besides, who would take care of the children? So I never got treatment.

I went to the police to request visas for us and to show them letters guaranteeing support and the request for our release. The police said I needed to wait. I loaded up the children and went to Bucharest thinking I would get to see Ceausescu and would request directly to leave the country. I went to the embassy but was told, "You are pretty bold or a little crazy." They calmed me down, and I returned home.

In a few months, during the time that Ilie was working with Senator Henry Jackson, the police called me to their office and gave me paperwork to fill out. I had to have all the children checked by the doctor, and it took another four to five months to complete the paperwork. After another two months, they called and told me to come and get the passports. I believe Senator Jackson's letter applied a lot of pressure to the authorities.

I was relieved that the passports had arrived, and I rejoiced in God's goodness. At the same time, I battled disappointment and frustration over money. As the effects of communism had taken control, the value of the lei had changed drastically and inflation had run rampant. Two thousand lei, an amount that at one time had meant three months salary was now only worth a few dollars. The authorities refused to pay me any more than two thousand lei for our home, land, and belongings. I was sickened that our home was sold for only $25.00. I felt helpless and inadequate, thinking that if a man were there to negotiate, more money would have been given to me.

However, a sense of urgency was running me. I packed up a few things we could carry and left without looking back. I was fearful they might change their minds and refuse to let us leave. I felt no sadness in leaving my home. I knew God had something much better for us. I had all my children and knew that Ilie was already safe. With each click of the train on the rails, my anxiety and fears melted away. I turned to the task of keeping the children entertained on our ride to a new life.

Once in Austria, the money from the home sale was just enough to pay the cab fare from the train station to the refugee camp.

IN THE COMPANY OF STRANGERS

In the morning, we met other Romanians, as well as a multitude of others from communist Eastern Block countries. Everyone had to stay there until the officials had the opportunity to take their interviews. Next, they would search records to make sure we weren't criminals. We had to wait there until we had permission to work or immigrate into a country willing to take us.

On the first day, I met a Romanian named George. Originally from Oradia, he had gotten to Italy on a passport while posing as a loyal communist. Like many, he had pretended his way through. In addition to the passport, he had papers and credentials. He was so happy for us and realized it was a miracle for us to be there without passports. Right then and there, we all prayed together, and George accepted Jesus in his heart!

The Lord told me that in three days I would be leaving. George overheard me telling Pete and Paul this, and he said, "I will follow. I will go with you."

Sure enough, I received word from God that I needed to leave and go to Austria. On the third day, I left the refugee camp and went with George to the train station. This was a huge step of faith for me. I really had to trust the Lord and believe that God really wanted me to do this. I hadn't, as of yet, received the proper paperwork to leave the refugee camp, and I didn't have a passport to move around the country or to cross the borders into other countries.

We found out when the next train was leaving for Austria, and George bought tickets for us both. It was a nice passenger train. It was the first time I had ever been on a luxury passenger train. Everyone had an assigned seat number and compartment. We boarded and went to our seats. A lady and two young men were in the same compartment. In speaking with them, we realized they were also Romanian. George told them how I had escaped from Romania and how I was on the train with no passport.

The lady's face was full of concern, as were the faces of the young men. She asked how I could be on the train without a passport and not be afraid. I told her that God had told me to do this, and I trusted in Him. She was a doctor, a psychiatrist, and she said that I must have something wrong with my brain. No one normal would do this. She asked how I talked with God. She said that she believed in God, but she had never heard of talking to God.

I told her, " I talk to God all the time. When I pray I believe that I am speaking to God. When I call Him "Father", I consider Him like my father. He listens to me and answers me. He teaches me, and He tells me what I need to do."

She said she had never heard of such a thing. "I think you have some mental problems," she said.

She and the young men talked amongst themselves, wondering how they could hide me. My seat was next to the window. They were to my right and in front of me. I assured them not to worry about me. I believed God had spoken to me, and I believed that they would see a miracle performed. They kept encouraging me to hide somewhere, under the seats perhaps. The heater was under the seats, and there was no room under them for a person.

I told them to be at peace because they were going to see God at work. Very soon the conductor was in our compartment to check our tickets. I gave him my ticket, and he checked mine and then the other tickets. After he left, I put my hand on my forehead and began to pray.

In the stillness I heard God say, "Do not fear. I will glorify My name, and they will not see you."

When the police came in to check passports, I remained silent and prayed. The police checked the passports of all the other people in the compartment and then left. The policeman didn't ask my name. It was as if he didn't even see me!

The lady in our compartment was amazed and spoke in a loud voice, "What kind of faith do you have? What kind of church do you go to? What kind of faith is this that men come and do not see you?"

George said, "See! I told you that God is with this man, and God is doing miracles through him! That is why I asked him to go with me to the refugee camp in Austria. The living conditions are a little better there."

As this conversation was dying down, the Austrian police came in to check passports. The first police check had been the Italian police. Again, I put my hand on my forehead and began to pray. Again, the police checked every passport in detail and never even noticed me sitting there!

"Praise be to God. God is with this man!" exclaimed the woman, after the police had left the compartment.

I began to weep with joy, and the lady clapped her hands. She and the two young men accepted Jesus Christ as their Lord and Savior before we arrived in Vienna, Austria, that day.

(At this point, Brother Ilie began to praise God saying, "God is good. He is good to me!

He is kind! He protects me! God can make you invisible so that no one can see you! I believe that was exactly the situation at that time.")

BIBLICAL AND LIFE APPLICATION

When God tells you to do something and you move out in faith to do it, it is important to speak and act in faith at all times. If I had boarded the train in faith and then faltered, I would have risked discovery. The spiritual shield surrounding me would have been weakened.

But he walked right through the crowd and went on his way. Luke 4:30 NIV

As I talked about in the last chapter, we have to operate in faith and trust. When God tells you to do something, you have to trust that He will bring it to pass just as He said. We have to believe that God will protect us as we step out in faith.

DISOBEDIENCE

I arrived in Vienna, Austria, with George. I had memorized an address of friends, Paul and Marcela, who lived there. Before setting out on foot to find my friends, George and I found a cheap hotel and stowed our luggage. After three or four hours of looking, we finally found out that the address was like an American post office box address at a post office. This was new to me. I didn't know people could have a post office box address. When I arrived at the post office and went inside, I expected to see Paul there.

I asked the people there, with the few German words I knew, "Where is Paul?" But no one even knew Paul.

They explained, "Paul doesn't live here. He lives at his home."

I asked, "Can you tell me where his home is?"

But they said, "It is not possible."

We waited in the post office for half a day for Paul to come. Finally, I wrote him a note and left it sticking out of his box. The note read, "I am free. We are here. We escaped from Romania! We are at a hotel here in Vienna!" We went back to the hotel and waited. We waited for three days, but Paul never came. So we decided (with persuasion from George) to find out what it would cost to purchase train tickets to Germany.

The lady and the young men from the train were heading on to Germany, and George wanted to travel with them. They, of course, had passports and could travel easily. Whenever you reached a free country, you could then ask for political asylum. The three were headed for the refugee camp in Germany because it was the best one in all of Europe. There you were supplied not only with clothing and toiletries, but also with money so you could send it back to your family. They would also place you in a class and teach you a new language.

I was very disappointed that Paul and Marcela hadn't come, and I was confused. I didn't understand why they hadn't responded to my note. George kept talking to me, telling me that we couldn't stay any longer. He was running out of money to pay for the two of us. Little by little, he convinced me to go on to Germany. The night before we were going to leave, I went to the train station to find out the train schedule. There were some people at the station speaking Romanian, so I asked them to get me the information about the trains. As I was speaking with them, I realized that the two men were well-educated.

One of them asked, "Are you the man who escaped from Romania? Is it true?"

I answered, "Yes, it is true."

He looked at me, smiled, and gave me his business card. It read "Director of Europe Free Radio." It seemed a miracle to me to meet him. He gave me his business card and some good advice.

He went with me to the information desk, got the information for me, and warned me that I had to be careful in Germany. If I were caught, the police might send me back to Romania. I began to be afraid, but he gave me the name, address, and phone number of his friend, who was a pastor in Munich.

I took the train information and headed back to the hotel. All the way back, I built up my faith. I told George what had happened, and we made our plans. We would have to take the train from Vienna to Salzburg, a three to four hour trip. From there, we would have to walk across the border on foot. We decided it was the best plan. From past experience, I knew that even when a situation seemed good, I still needed to pray. In prayer the Holy Spirit warned me not to go with George. I felt I should go to the refugee camp in Trischirken, Austria, (Trischirken means three churches).

I told George what I thought the Lord had told me, and he cried and insisted that I come with him. He kept saying, "Come with me. I have friends there. They can help you and help get your family out of Romania. Please come with me."

Even though I had prayed and knew the Lord's will, and even after walking in miracle after miracle, I gave in to George's insistence and chose to go against God's wishes. I would live to regret that decision.

BIBLICAL AND LIFE APPLICATION

When you are walking close to the Lord, you know when you aren't going in the right direction. There is a distinct uneasiness in your spirit. The Holy Spirit is, at that time, witnessing to your spirit.

...We know it by the Spirit He gave us. 1 John 3:24b NIV

When we read how the Israelites turned their back on God and wanted to return to Egypt, we wonder how they can be thinking this way. Yet in this case, I knew the path I was supposed to take, and I purposely went another direction.

...You are just like your fathers: You always resist the Holy Spirit! Acts 7:51b NIV

Walking by faith demands discipline. It demands blocking out the negative and only listening to the positive voice of God.

He will die for lack of discipline, led astray by his own great folly. Proverbs 5:23 NKJV

Satan can use people, as much as circumstances, to derail our walk with God. Manipulation, which can take the form of whining, crying, and threatening, is a tool the devil uses to change our minds. In my case, I gave in to George's constant whining and crying. What looked on the surface to be genuine concern for my well-being was, in fact, a trap being set by Satan.

The story of Samson in Judges 16 is a perfect example of what happens when we give in to manipulation. Samson knew that his hair was never to be cut. It was a covenant between him and God; yet he gave into the whining of Delilah. This cost Samson his strength and his direct connection to God. He was captured, but God in His mercy allowed Samson's hair to grow again. In the end, it gave him the strength needed to destroy the enemy. Samson died in the process. Though God liberally gives us mercy, there are still consequences to our actions.

TROUBLE ABOUNDS

The next day George and I went to the train station and bought the tickets from Vienna to Salzburg. When we got off the train at Salzburg, we started on foot towards the border, but someone told us that the distance to the border was very far away. We decided to take a taxi. The taxi took us about two hundred meters from the border. There was a forest close by, and we walked into it, picking our way towards the border. It was already dark, and a slushy rain and snow mix began falling.

At the border crossing, there was a soldier with a machine gun and guard dog. We sat at the edge of the clearing, hiding behind the trees. I was praying hard, but I still hadn't seen the light that guided me out of Romania. In my heart, I knew what we were doing was not the best thing. I knew I was disobeying the plan God had for me. I had given in to George's insistence and couldn't shake the feeling that things were about to go very, very wrong.

We waited until the soldier and dog passed us again. When he was ten to fifteen meters away, we ran across the border. He was so close to us when we passed him! However, he never heard us, and the dog never smelled us.

We hiked out of the forest and found ourselves near the Autobahn, the German highway system. George ran out to the road and began to hail cars, making a sign that he wanted to hitchhike. That was the big mistake because the car he hailed turned out to be a German police car. They stopped, and when we realized they were policemen, we started running back into the woods. The police got on their radios and called for more police and dogs to come. There we were, in the forest at night, in the rain, being chased by police and dogs. We were in a country where, if caught, they would probably send us back to Romania. I knew better. I should have listened to God.

We stumbled onto a creek and went down into the water. It was incredibly cold, and the water went up to our waists. By the time the police reached the creek, we had already climbed the opposite bank and melted into the woods on the other side. The dogs lost our scent, and the police eventually gave up the chase. George and I walked on through the forest for another hour or so until we came upon a small village named Peiding. We were deep in a disagreement as to whether or not we were in Austria or Germany. George was sure we were still in Austria. I was sure we were in Germany. There was a gas station at the edge of town. There I proved to George that we were in Germany. The gas prices were written in German marks rather than in Austrian shillings.

There were some men at the gas station, and I asked where the train station was located. I could say a few words in German, and the men pointed and talked. Among us all, we figured out what direction and how far the train station was from Peiding, and off we went. The station was very small and had just one man working. He was the conductor, as well as ticket agent. George bought our tickets to Munich. The cost was sixteen marks per ticket.

We were so cold and soaked through from the rain and the creek that we sat right next to the radiator. We were going to have a long wait. George got bored and went to talk with the man who sold us the tickets. Soon George was sharing with him that we had escaped from Romania. I went over and grabbed George by the arm to stop him from talking.

I asked him, "What did you do? Why did you tell him that?"

George tried to push me away saying, "So what? He doesn't care."

At that moment, I saw the man pick up the phone. Within two minutes the police were there, and we were arrested and taken to jail as if we were big criminals.

We were hauled away in handcuffs, interviewed, and fingerprinted. Because I had no papers, it was very important during my interview that I stick to the story told to the Italian police—one change in the story would have resulted in my deportation back to Romania.

George, on the other hand, was terrified. He was so scared that his hair turned white overnight. When I saw him in the morning, I couldn't believe it. He was so nervous that he kept changing his story. This made them ask him even more questions.

They finally put us in a dark cell. George spent the time hitting himself and blaming himself for foolishly talking at the station.

He kept whining over and over, "Pray. Pray and see what God shows you. See if these guys are going to send us back to Romania."

I would tell him that I had peace; God wouldn't let us down. Secretly I, too, was afraid. I had been disobedient. God had told me to go to the refugee camp in Austria, and I had not listened. Poor George. The stress really messed up his body, and he started having stomach problems as well.

For two weeks, they interviewed and interrogated us. The police brought in an older man, a Romanian who lived in the area, to translate what we were saying. I received a lot of favor with this man and the police. They would only interrogate me for a few minutes and then send me back to my cell. They kept interrogating George because his story kept changing.

The older man even told George he was in trouble because his story kept changing. He gave him an example. "When you first arrived and before you were searched, you were asked if you had any money. You said, 'No,' but the police found three thousand Deutsch marks hidden in your shoe."

So the police lost trust in George because they caught him in lies. For twenty-one days they kept us locked up. They were very harsh with us because of George.

They would let us go outside into the courtyard for an hour each day. Normally, they were supposed to let us out for three hours a day. The odor of the prisoners made it hard to stay inside the jail. Some people from Hungary, who had done some very bad things, were among the prisoners. In another room, there were forty prisoners in one cell.

(Again, Brother Ilie stopped for a moment, overwhelmed by the memory. He was praying, "Oh, dear Lord, thank you that I don't remember that smell day and night.")

After twenty-one days, they loaded us in a van with Hungarians and Yugoslavians and sent us off. The van had no windows, and to scare us, they told us that they were sending us back to Romania.

After a little over an hour, they stopped somewhere, opened the door, and called our names. As we got out of the van, they closed the door and drove off. It truly was a miracle that God had caused, and we could see it with our own eyes. We had been returned to Salzburg! We were put in jail for one month while the police sorted out what had happened. It was much easier there than at the jail in Germany. The time went by very slowly, and I spent my days teaching George from the Bible and learning some German.

After a month, they took us to the refugee camp. They granted us political asylum and all the rights that went with it. We were to be quarantined on the fourth floor in a lock up for four to six weeks while they checked our identities, where we were from, and our stories. After a time, they would give us papers and more freedom, along with the ability to immigrate to a different country or to get work in the area.

About one week into the verification process, I had a dream about Paul. I dreamed that we had gone to his post office box and from there to a stream to fish. I looked for Paul at the stream but could not find him. He was in the United States. It was a strange dream.

The next day, I told George and others that I thought I was going to be free shortly. They all laughed and said it wasn't possible. I hadn't been there long enough. They said I had only been there for a week, and others had been there for over three weeks. They explained to me the procedure was that after four weeks I would be interviewed.

After dinner I was walking down the hallway. I saw Paul and another man coming towards me. At first I thought it was a vision. I turned to the people I was with and asked if anyone could see people walking towards us. They all replied that they could and identified one of the men as the director of the refugee camp. They didn't understand why he was there. They said the director was seldom seen at the camp.

Paul had found my note and had come looking for me. The

director took me to his office, and I was interviewed the same evening. That very night I went home with Paul. Finally free.

BIBLICAL AND LIFE APPLICATION

Even though we make mistakes and don't obey God, in His grace, He watches over us. God told me to go to the refugee camp in Austria. George spoke when he shouldn't have, but God, in His grace, allowed us to arrive in Germany. God's plan could not be fulfilled because we didn't have the patience and wisdom needed to do what He had told us to do. These two very important points need to be at work in our lives:

1) We need to have patience.

2) We need to have wisdom.

My son, preserve sound judgment and discernment, do not let them out of your sight; they will be life for you, an ornament to grace your neck. Then you will go on your way in safety, and your foot will not stumble. Proverbs 3:21-23 NIV

We have to learn to wait and trust God in faith. Everything that God starts, He will bring to completion. He doesn't start and only do seventy-five percent or ninety-nine percent, but He does one hundred percent of everything He starts.

Wait for the Lord; be strong and take heart and wait for the Lord. Psalm 27:14 NIV

George spoke to people around him, and in doing so we were caught. The Bible tells us, in many verses, to have the wisdom and discipline to hold our tongues. The old phrase "Loose lips sink ships" applies in this situation.

A fool's lips bring him strife, and his mouth invites a beating. A fool's mouth is his undoing, and his lips are a snare to his soul. Proverbs 18:6-7 NIV

At one time or another, each one of us falls into the category of the fool. We must guard our mouths, as much as we guard our hearts, to ensure that we don't fall into the snare these verses speak of.

Section Three
The Promise of America

He who dwells in the secret place
of the Most High
shall abide under the shadow
of the Almighty.
I will say of the Lord, "He is my
refuge and my fortress,
My God, in whom I trust."
Psalm 91:1 NKJV

KIDNAPPED!

Pain. There it was again. Pain in his side. What was that? Again and again, it was beginning to feel as if someone was kicking him in the side, knocking the wind out of him. Whoever was doing this was serious and meant business. He tried to open his eyes, but they would not open. What is wrong, he wondered, as yet another kick landed on his ribs. Again, he tried to open his eyes while raising his head. Whatever was affecting his eyes was also affecting his head and neck because none of his muscles and limbs seemed to be operating.

Another swift kick to the ribs sent shock waves to his brain as he struggled to function. He desperately knew that he needed to wake up. Something was wrong, terribly wrong. He had felt it in his spirit just before falling asleep. He remembered eating and getting very sleepy, but under all of that had been an overwhelming anxiousness that something was wrong. Unfortunately, he had fallen asleep, dead to the world, before having the opportunity to figure out what it was.

Surely his companions would help, he thought, as yet another kick landed on his now bruised ribs. Harder than before, this one jolted him enough to pop his eyes open. He struggled to keep them open. Blinking big, eye-widening blinks, he surveyed his surroundings.

He was still in the van, but the shades had all been drawn closed. His so-called companions were nowhere to be seen. Vomit covered the front of his shirt, and he moved to get clear of the remaining mess.

By now the Holy Spirit was thundering in his mind, "WAKE UP! DANGER!"

His struggle to function reached a frantic pitch. He could hear voices outside, and he began to pound on the side of the vehicle and yell for help in German. He could hear concerned voices and the beginnings of a rescue attempt. The Holy Spirit continued to impress on him that time was short and danger was very near. The message pounded in his mind hard and fast, keeping pace with the pounding of his heart. The door suddenly sprang open and hands reached in to pull him out. Ilie struggled to his feet, as the Austrian police arrived on the scene.

Quickly assessing the situation, the police loaded him in their car. As they were pulling out of the parking lot, a large, black, official-looking car passed, and he could feel the evil flowing from it. Ilie shuddered as he recognized that evil from his past, and he rebuked it by name. Whatever danger had been planned, it had been in that car.

Ilie struggled to turn around and see who got out of the car, but the car had quickly turned around and sped away in the opposite direction. Ilie settled back in the seat. Breathing a sigh of relief, he offered a silent prayer of thanksgiving. Whatever Satan had attempted had once again been thwarted by God's grace. Ilie was still safe in the Master's hand.

FREEDOM BRINGS NEW CHALLENGES

I lived at Paul's house with his family, and I learned how to print Bibles and Christian literature on his printing press. These materials were later sent into communist countries through smuggling rings. In the six months I worked with Paul, I was able to send many things back into Romania to my family—food, clothes, and money that helped Aurica care for the children. The money was always hidden inside food. Once, I hid a wad of money inside a large jar of jam, and another time, inside some chocolate.

I knew that these items were a huge blessing to the family and helped ease the stress of being in Romania alone. This bounty, coupled with what she had from the farm, gave her more than when I had been working there! God was providing so much that Aurica was able to help other families who lived nearby. With God, my family lacked nothing during this time.

Once I received a passport and my political asylum was finalized, I was free to move about in sixteen countries without a special visa. God opened the door for me to travel to Denmark, and there I spent time with a family I met in Austria. Benton and his family had worked at Paul's mission for a time.

While I was there, God gave me a word for him. The word was that God was going to lift him up and put him in a high place, a very important place. He would serve some very high officials. True to God's word, the day came when Benton was placed in a new position. He was in charge of security for Queen Margrethe of Denmark!

While I was in Denmark, I worked for a Baptist brother who had a large farm. While working there, I had a vision for this brother. In the vision, someone who worked for him on the farm was taking drugs and wasn't right mentally. He was, in fact, insane. God showed me this man's mind, and I saw that he wanted to start a fire at the farm. In the vision, I saw that God had stopped the fire. I shared what God had shown me with this brother, and I received much favor from him. God impressed on his heart to help me bring my family out of Romania. He wanted my family to immigrate to Denmark, and he wanted to provide us with a home and everything we would need. But I shared with him what God had placed in my heart, and the knowledge that my home was in America. I also told him that I was open to God's will for us. I remained in prayer, and after a short time, I received a letter from the American Embassy in Austria.

In the letter, they wanted to know how I was and what my plans were. Was I planning to stay in Europe? Was I going on to America? If I was going to America, I had to do it within a certain length of time or my rights to immigrate there would be lost. Immediately, I wrote back that I wanted to go to America. Shortly after that, I received a phone call saying that I needed to return to Austria for my final exit interview in late January.

My Baptist brother was disappointed that I was leaving, but I reminded him that I had to do God's will. My time in Denmark had been good, and I had used the time to gather sponsorship letters from friends in Los Angeles, Chicago, Detroit, New York, and Florida.

As usual, the enemy tried to dissuade me. I received a letter from someone in Chicago who told me that it would be better to remain in Denmark. They said Chicago had lots of problems and hard times. They said I would regret coming to America for the rest of my life. This was the first letter I got back, and I was discouraged. However, every other letter I received was pouring forth with promise and encouragement. I was built up through these letters, and I prayed, asking God for direction. God told me that I needed to go to California.

In my meeting with the ambassador, I told him I wanted to go to California. They bought my ticket and sent me to Los Angeles. A Romanian brother in Los Angeles sponsored me, and I lived with him and his family. But my heart was grieved because I didn't know how things were going with my family. Aurica had heard that I had made it to America, and she was upset because she had just handed in all the paperwork to go to Denmark.

When I called her and told her I was in America, she said, "My goodness, what have you done?" I assured her and encouraged her that God wanted me to go to America.

After a month in America, I had another dream. In the dream a man came to me with a gold key. I didn't know the man. He told me the key would allow the door to open for my family to come to America. When I woke up I had a name on my mind—Jackson. The very next day, I called a friend, Pavel Balos, who had been in America for a few years. I told him my dream and how I had felt in the dream that I should write to a man named Jackson.

Pavel knew about a senator named Henry Jackson, who had played a key role in signing the most favored nation status for Romania in 1970. He carried weight and could apply pressure to the Romanian government to possibly release my family. I wrote to him, and Pavel helped translate the letter for me. In short, I told Senator Jackson how I had escaped with God's help. I also told him that I had been forced to leave behind my wife and seven children, who were waiting for an opening to leave the country and join me.

Within two weeks, I had received a response from him. I was full of joy and tears as I read his promise to do what he could to help. I waited for several days before calling Aurica. When I reached her she was very upset and discouraged. She said the police refused to listen to her when she talked about coming to America. I gave her a word of encouragement. I told her that anything God started He would finish. He never did anything seventy-five percent or ninety-nine percent, but He always did one hundred percent. Just as the last word left my mouth, we were disconnected.

I continued to keep my "line" open to God, and I continued to pray and trust in the Lord. I sent a second letter to the senator. I received another letter back from him stating that he had information on my family, and within the next week, they should receive their visas and their situation would be resolved. I believed his words. Through tears of joy, I gave all the glory to God. Sure enough, within one week, Aurica called to say that she didn't know what had happened, but the police had given her passports. She and the children had to leave Romania as soon as possible. I told her that God's plans were always brought to completion.

Aurica and the children left Romania and were sent to the refugee camp in Austria. They were held there while applying to come to America. Sometimes it could take up to two years to gain the privilege to immigrate to the United States.

In the meantime, I explained to friends that my family had been sent to Austria. I wanted to go to them, but I was told it was impossible as I had only been in America for a few months. I trusted God and went to the Immigration Office. I waited in a very long line. The line literally had a couple hundred people in it. When I finally got to talk to someone, it was all negative.

I went back the next day and arrived very early, around 3:00 a.m. I was one of the first in line. I insisted on seeing the director and was told it wasn't possible. I was told that I had to make an appointment sixty days in advance.

I said, "No. No. I need it now."

The secretary kept saying, "No."

I kept saying, "Yes. I'm praying."

Finally, the secretary sent me to another secretary on the third floor. She said the same thing, "You can't speak to the director, but maybe you could talk with one of the managers."

I said, "Listen, I have a family, a wife and seven children, who have been released from Romania and are at the refugee camp in Austria. I need to go to them and help them. Think of my family. I haven't seen them in almost two years. My children are probably crying."

She kept refusing me, but I didn't leave. Tears began to run down my face, and I couldn't stop them. It was as if all the pent up emotions of being separated from my family were pouring out in a public display that I couldn't stop. It was frustrating and embarrassing at the same time. The secretary stepped into another room, spoke to someone, and came back out. She asked me to return in one hour.

I returned in one hour, and she took me upstairs to the highest director. He was originally from Switzerland and had immigrated a number of years earlier. He told me to go with the secretary to have my picture taken and then return to him after that was done. Within an hour, I had a white passport with a green line through it.

No one could believe I had gotten the passport. All of my friends pitched in to help cover the cost of the plane ticket. I flew right away to Austria. I arrived at night and went straight to the refugee camp. Many of my children were already asleep. My baby, of course, didn't know me and was a little afraid of me at first. The director of the refugee camp was there, and he was amazed to see me. He was afraid I had made a big mistake, and that I wouldn't be able to leave again.

I explained that I had a white passport, and he said, "That's impossible."

I just smiled and said, "With God all things are possible." To satisfy the director, we went to the embassy the next day to be sure my papers were in order.

They said, "If the officials there gave you this passport, then that means you have great favor. They trust you, and you are legal to remain in Europe for up to one year."

I have never met anyone who has heard of any other person having such an experience with the Immigration Department. This favor meant that I was able to stay and visit with my wife and children.

My wife was a bit sick when she arrived, and I thought she had bronchitis. A few months before my family was scheduled to be released, I returned to the States to prepare for their arrival. About the time they were to leave, the doctors came and told Aurica that she had to stay behind in isolation while they treated her for tuberculosis. The children were brought into America with another lady, who had been at the refugee camp.

When I learned that Aurica had to stay behind, I remembered what she always said when stressed or tired. "Lord, I want to have a few days alone, somewhere in the forest, away from the kids, where I can be quiet and rest."

My darling Aurica had to stay at the sanitarium for four months. The sanitarium was actually a retreat center set in the mountain woodlands. Poor Aurica! She lived at that lovely resort, alone in the woods, where it was quiet and peaceful. She received exactly what she had prayed for!

She cried a lot during that time. It was hard to be away from her family. It was hard to think that everyone had begun their new life in America, and she had been left behind. Yet God, in His grace and mercy, loved her so much that He set aside that special time just for her!

The children arrived, and life in America became full again. We were blessed to live in a brand new house that no one had ever lived in, and we were living there rent-free! For the first time in their lives, my children were able to see a refrigerator—full of food. There was an abundance of fruit—bananas, oranges, and apples. It was a great blessing to us. All of the children started school, except the baby, and began to learn English. Within a few months, they spoke English better than I did.

And God blessed us in America, many blessings on and on.

BIBLICAL AND LIFE APPLICATION

Many times, God has spoken to me and told me to never disconnect from Him. He said to keep my "phone line" open to Him, in order to keep the communication open between us. If our communication line with God is disconnected, then the enemy will come and bring discouragement and fear. That's why God wants us to have a clear connection with Him. Every time we hear and listen to His voice, we will be encouraged, lifted up, and strengthened.

He who has ears, let him hear. Matthew 11:15 NKJV

People around me kept telling me that I would never be given a visa to leave America so soon after my arrival. Nevertheless, I moved forward by faith, and God opened the doors for me. When the camp director questioned my arrival, I spoke by faith and quoted scripture to him. Satan can't fight against the Word.

Always use God's word to do your battles. This is why it is so important that you know God's word for yourself. There is a quote, I can't remember who said it, "Never dig up in disbelief what you have sown by faith." As you move forward in faith, always remain steadfast in your faith. Never give Satan room to maneuver.

...With man this is impossible, but with God all things are possible. Matthew 19:26b NIV

Instead, when I arrived at the embassy, I was told that I had great favor. As we walk in obedience to God, favor comes to us. I would rather have one minute of God's favor than a year of man's favor!

It is written "*...the Lord bestows favor and honor; no good thing does he withhold from those whose walk is blameless.*" Psalm 84:11b NIV

Aurica always dreamed of some time to rest, and when stressed, she would ask God for some time alone. Though Aurica's time alone may not have come at a time that she thought was good, God in His wisdom knew exactly when she would need it and arranged it for her. God loved her so much that He orchestrated a special retreat just for her! God loves each one of us with that same love. If you will let Him, He can orchestrate special things for you too.

Aurica's Journal

When I finally arrived at the refugee camp with all the children, I was exhausted. Trying to keep track of the children in a sea of people was a daunting task. In those days people watched out and cared for each other's children as if they were their own. I know that there were many other arms and laps employed to help care for my children.

Within days, all the children had again been checked and found to be healthy. They were ready to travel as soon the paperwork was complete. The doctors found a black spot the size of a nickel, on my lung. It was the same spot that had been there before Iliuta was born, and they immediately started me on medication.

Ilie arrived from America, and we had a joyous reunion. We had two weeks together before he had to return to California. Finally in December 1976, the paperwork was complete, and it was time to leave. I was examined again, only to find that the medication hadn't worked. The spot was still there.

There was a young lady who had been wonderful at helping me with the children at the camp. Fortunately, she was released to go to America at the same time. She escorted all my children across the sea to freedom. I went with them to the airport, kissed each child good-bye, and watched the plane fly off into the distance. Then I was taken by car to a sanitarium for further treatment for tuberculosis.

I was very sad. I hadn't had time alone, without at least one or two children around, for so many years that I didn't know what to do with myself. At times, the silence was deafening. They told me that I would need three to four months of these treatments, and if I would work at resting, I would soon be in America. There was a time when the thought that rest would be work was unfathomable. Yet now, as months stretched before me without anyone to care for, I realized that it would be work not to fret or to pick up someone's load, and just focus on me. I spent my time praying and reading my Bible. I hadn't had such abundant time since I was a young girl, and I relished my time with the Lord.

I worked on my English with a teacher who came each evening to teach those going to America. The teacher would hold up pictures and tell us the word for the picture. We would all repeat the word. Learning a new language at my age was a challenge!

I stayed at the sanitarium for six weeks. Then I was taken to a beautiful resort hotel near Innsbruck, Austria, high up in the mountains and nestled in a forest. There were many immigrants waiting to leave. They had come from Albania, Turkey, Bulgaria, Czechoslovakia, Romania, Yugoslavia, and Russia. I made friends with some other Romanian women there, and we would go for long walks through the woods. I walked and talked without a care in the world! The hotel gave me three wonderful meals each day, new clothes, and even spending money! Ilie would call every day to check on me. I was having a wonderful holiday created by God just for me!

I was allowed to go to America on April 21, 1977. I was so excited to be entering America, my new country.

LIFE BEGINS ANEW

So here we were in this new country, so different from where I grew up. I had a new beginning. I began working to take care of my family. I had to work more than one job, full and part-time jobs, to make ends meet. In 1976, I also started a Romanian New Testament church with about five families in Bell Flower, California. I had asked the Lord what I should be doing because I had a great desire to serve the Lord. I couldn't see much that I could do besides meet with, pray with, and teach these few families.

God clearly showed me that for the first three years I needed to be their pastor, their teacher, and their servant. So that was the way we started out. Soon a lot more people were coming. Through the church, we began to sponsor many families that wanted to immigrate to the United States from the refugee camps. They came to us from Italy, Yugoslavia, Austria, Germany, and Romania. Within a year, our church had grown to around two hundred people!

I was very, very busy because I was working full-time to care for my family, and all of my extra time was spent taking care of different families that had immigrated to the States.

Soon six years had gone by. I believed the Lord had spoken very clearly to me to pastor, teach, and lead for three years, yet I had gone over that time by three years. As a result, it was a very difficult time for me. I was exhausted. Sometimes I felt very weak, like I couldn't do anything. I was exhausted in every way—mentally, physically, spiritually, and emotionally.

God spoke to me. From the beginning, He had spoken to me to be in that place for three years—not six. Instead I had listened to people. The people wanted me to stay and continue the work I had been doing. I had listened to them and learned a valuable lesson. When we listen to people more than we listen to God, we get into a place where we will be very tired and exhausted.

In the first days of January 1980, I made a decision to wait on the Lord without any predetermined time frame or limit of days in prayer and fasting. Almost at once, a series of trials and attacks came against us. All of my children, one by one, came down with different illnesses. My wife had some kind of skin infection. I found myself in the hospital. I had fallen unconscious, and when I came to, I was in the hospital hooked up to all kinds of equipment. The doctors found out I had high blood pressure and some heart problems.

I continued fasting and praying as I went through trial after trial. Through it, I learned to draw from an even deeper well of faith. That faith would be tested in April 1980, when the greatest trial of my life came, and there was a time when I didn't think I would ever recover.

BIBLICAL AND LIFE APPLICATION

Even Jesus drew away by Himself for a time of refreshing and renewal. The people pulled and demanded much of His power and strength. In my disobedience, I had allowed the world to drain me of my strength, both physical and spiritual. In my attempt to stay and be a help to God's people, I probably ended up not helping them much at all, since I was not operating at the capacity that I could have been.

Sometimes we allow ourselves to think that "nobody can do it as good as me" or that "there's no one else to take my place." Who are we to think that God won't bring someone else that is capable of doing the job, or that He doesn't already have someone in place to take over? In fact, who are we to think that there isn't someone who can do it BETTER than we can?

As I finally came to grips with the need to step aside, the groundwork preparation of ending one thing and starting another began. This process of death and birth is as true in biblical things as it is in nature. The job of pastoring had to die. Then there was a birthing process (any mother will tell you that birthing has pain) where new thoughts, ideas, vitality, and a new vision was brought forth.

In a way, my illness and lack of strength was directly related to my lack of vision. Since God had originally told me that my pastorate would last three years, the vision for that pastorate had been a three-year vision. I was literally perishing for lack of a new, clear vision for the future.

Where there is no vision, the people perish...
Proverbs 29:18a KJV

Aurica's Journal

Oh taste and see that the Lord is good! We were so blessed as we entered America! God provided a brand new, four-bedroom house for us to live in. A dentist had built the house, but it had never sold. We were able to live there rent-free for a time as we got adjusted to life in freedom.

Everything was new. Instead of dirt or wood floors, I had soft white carpet for the children to play on. Where I had once made meals on a wood-burning stove, now I had a cooking stove with an oven. It was a dream kitchen, and I had to learn how to cook all over again! Before I had no refrigerator to keep things cool, now I could keep things cool and keep other things frozen! Instead of hauling the family clothes in a wheelbarrow to the river and washing them by hand, I now had a washer and dryer to do it for me. Oranges, once considered an expensive luxury that I would ration among the children by giving each child one slice a day, could now literally be picked off our own tree in the backyard!

Eventually, we bought a small house of our own with one bedroom. We converted the garage into a bedroom for all the children. We lived there for two years and then sold it. We then bought a four-bedroom house with a swimming pool near Anaheim, California. We added two more bedrooms onto the side, as well as expanding the tiny kitchen.

Ilie worked in maintenance cleaning, in addition to pastoring a church for Romanian immigrants. He cleaned offices for large companies: vacuuming, dusting, mopping, polishing, etc. When the older children came home from school, they would pile in the car with Ilie, and off they would go to work. They would work as a team from 5:00 p.m. to 8:00 p.m. each day. Ilie would bring home about one thousand dollars per building.

When we first arrived in America, we were able to go to the store with fifty dollars and buy all the food we needed for the week. My, how times have changed! Ilie never received any money for pastoring the church. We sponsored many families to come to America. They would come and stay with us for two to three weeks while we helped them find a home to rent, get their licenses, find furniture, and in general, integrate them into the community. Most people needed a translator, and all of us, including the children, were sent to translate for them. We were able to help many families, and God was faithful to meet our needs during this time.

Between 1978 and 1985, we sponsored and helped over one hundred families find a new life of freedom in America.

ILIUTA, CHILD OF GOD

The biggest trial for us all started in late April 1980. I can't say we weren't warned. At the time, it just hadn't seemed like a possibility. My youngest son, Iliuta; my daughter, Lidia; and I all had similar dreams within a few days of each other.

Lidia dreamed that Jesus came to our house and picked the most beautiful flower from our garden. Lidia was disappointed that He had chosen the prettiest one and asked why he was taking that flower. Jesus, in the dream, had replied, "Because I love this flower very much." Then He broke the flower and took it.

Iliuta dreamed that a black bowl had hit him straight on, and the moment that he was hit, he began to fly. I dreamed that Iliuta was surrounded by light, and he was being lifted towards heaven. At the time, I understood that something was about to take place in his life, but I didn't realize the extent.

The day of the accident, we had a family staying with us that we had sponsored to come to America. They hadn't found a place to live yet, so they and their seven children were living with Aurica and I, and our seven children. We had gone to get groceries, and our son, Sam, had taken some of the children to the park to play.

We hadn't been at the store long when I felt the Holy Spirit impressing me, "Go home, immediately. Something has happened."

I urged the women to grab only what was needed, and we rushed home as quickly as possible. I felt that something was terribly wrong. I was weak all over and felt as if I had been shot with a bullet in my heart.

When we arrived at home, all of the children were crying and told me that Iliuta was in an accident and was at the hospital. We left immediately, and when we got there, they wouldn't let us go into the emergency room. We were told that they were operating on him. No one wanted to tell us how badly he was hurt or what the situation was. At that moment, I was reminded of a good doctor friend of mine that was a specialist named Dr. Lou. I called him thinking I would only catch his secretary because he was never in the office. However, this time he answered the phone. I told him what was going on, and he was there within a few minutes.

Dr. Lou was able to go into the operating room and work with the doctors. He asked if I wanted to go in, too, but I felt that I should stay out. I stayed in the hallway praying with my wife. Within a few minutes, I saw a vision. A choir of angels descended in a circle and surrounded Iliuta. In a few moments they rose, still in a circle, with Iliuta in the center. They flew towards heaven.

(Brother Ilie said at this point that it was hard for him to talk about this. He was reliving those moments as he was speaking to us.)

About thirty minutes later, Dr. Lou came out of the emergency room and told us that Iliuta was gone. At that moment, I was very sad, very hurt, and very wounded.

I began to argue with God and say, "God, why did you allow this to happen?"

God said, "This is my plan."

One day, when I was weeping bitterly for my little Iliuta, God reminded me of another time that I had wept bitterly. I had been at a prayer meeting in Timisoara. I had fallen down in the Spirit and was out for a couple of hours.

During that time, an angel visited me and said, "Come with me for a second. I want to reveal and show you some things."

As soon as the angel had touched my arm, I saw many wonderful things. When I woke from the visit with the angel, I had wept bitterly.

I had felt so sad and asked, "Why do I have to come back from such a beautiful place?"

And so to comfort me now, the Lord reminded me of that experience and said, "For just one second I took you and showed you all of the wonderful things that I have prepared for you, and you didn't want to return. Why are you weeping for your son whom I decided to bring home with me forever? You don't have the right to cry. I entrusted this child to you for just a short period of time, and you don't have the right to argue with me and cry over him."

God reminded me of another experience I'd had in 1963, and the memory began to calm me down. That incident had happened on November 22, 1963, the day J. F. Kennedy was assassinated. At that time, God had comforted me with the words, "I have taken him (JFK) to be with me."

And so the Lord began to comfort me with His words, "I have taken your son to be with Me because I have loved him. I want to show him My glory. He is precious to me. I know I took something precious. Know that I have a great plan that you do not know and cannot understand at this time. It will be hard to comprehend, but I will do a great work through this."

It was one of the first funerals for a Romanian in California, especially a child. Many, many Romanians came to the funeral, and God moved on the hearts of young people. Many were touched by God's power. Many young people made decisions to come closer and serve God. I remember that Pastor Paul, from the Foursquare Church, preached from Romans 8:28. In this scripture, the Bible shows us God's sovereignty. He's in charge of all things, and all things work together for good to those who love and trust Him.

It was a very hard trial, a testing time for my family and me. But victory was the Lord's because He comforted us. Many brothers and sisters, from area churches, surrounded us. They visited us, blessed us, brought us food, and other things that we needed. We never felt alone. God's family surrounded us.

The Lord used this time to reveal to me that my time as a pastor was going to come to an end very quickly. I began to feel more peace of mind and more of a release. I felt like a heavy yoke was being lifted off my shoulders.

BIBLICAL AND LIFE APPLICATION

We can never fully understand why God allows lives to be taken. No matter what happens, we cannot blame God or harbor anger against God. If we do so, we only open the door for Satan to come in and steal more things that are precious to us.

Be self-controlled and alert. Your enemy the devil prowls around like a roaring lion looking for someone to devour. 1 Peter 5:8 NIV

The Bible tells us that children are a gift that only He can give. *...God has presented me with a precious gift...*Genesis 30:20a NIV

We must love our children while they are ours and pour into them everything they will need to survive. Then we must trust God—no matter what—with the rest.

We had gone to the store that day with another couple that we had sponsored into the country. Americans take for granted the abundance of choices and supplies at the grocery stores. The first time I went to the store in America was a very heady experience. It was almost more than I could handle—the sights, the smells, the abundance, and the colors. You didn't have to stand in line to get one thing you desperately needed, but instead, there was such abundance and so many choices available. It was easy to get "happy" and take way more than was needed. We were used to grabbing as much of whatever was available as we could. At first, it was hard to understand that when we returned in a few days or a week later, the same amount of product or more would be available to us.

The children had gone to the park to play. In those days, parents didn't have to worry about children being kidnapped or hurt. The world was a different place then. Samuel was in charge, and they headed out as a group with Iliuta in tow. They went to the playground at the school, but the grounds were closed. They decided to go to the city park, which was on the other side of Beach Boulevard. Beach Boulevard was a six-lane highway where the speed limit was fifty miles per hour. Iliuta ran out in front of a car while attempting to keep up with the older children.

When we came home, Samuel and the other children were waiting for us at the door. All of the children were upset and crying, and they told us that a car had hit Iliuta. They said his collarbone was broken. We left immediately for the hospital and waited in the emergency room for word. I was able to see him through a crack in the door, and he was in horrible condition, bloody and swollen.

Ilie went and called a doctor friend, Dr. Lou, who was a heart specialist, to see if there was anything he could do or a doctor he could recommend. Within minutes, Dr. Lou was at the hospital and went into the emergency room to help.

Ilie and I stayed in the waiting room and prayed. While we

were praying, Ilie had another vision of angels gathering around Iliuta on the table, and the angels took him, ascending up and up as far as the eye could see. While he was telling me the details of the vision, the doctor came to tell us that Iliuta was gone.

Iliuta died in April 1980. We all suffered great pain and sorrow at this loss. The pain of losing a child is tremendous and indescribable. It is like a deep hole of pain that lives in your heart, and you have it with you every day. I wasn't aware that Ilie was struggling with God at this point. We were, by the grace of God, unlike some couples that drift apart while grieving. We actually came closer together, not only as husband and wife but our children came closer as well. We clung to each other for strength and support. Together, as a unit, we clung to God and His promises.

God was merciful to protect Samuel from guilt and condemnation. He struggled with it a little, but it didn't stay with him. Slowly Ilie gave his anger over to God and began to be healed. The other children slowly began to recuperate as well. Only Daniel held on to his anger and began to have problems. I prayed that God would give me another child to fill the hole in my heart, and God in His goodness responded.

I became pregnant again, and nine months later Betty was born. I was so happy and excited. I spent all day, every day, thanking God for this new gift. I was never sick and never had any pain. Betty was my tenth child, born in 1981. She was cute and good, and she was never, ever sick. She was a healthy, beautiful child, and God healed my pain for Iliuta through Betty.

Six months to the day after Iliuta was struck and killed, another Romanian child that we had sponsored to America was struck and killed at the same intersection. She was the same age that Iliuta had been. The city mourned again for the loss of a child.

ANGELS WITH PARACHUTES

After being released from pastoring, I began traveling and ministering in the refugee camps again. I traveled through Italy, Yugoslavia, Austria, and Germany. I would go into the camps, preach the Gospel, and encourage the people there. I would pray with them and bring them Bibles. I continued doing this until Romania became a free country in 1989. I was working full-time in ministry and working part-time to cover our living expenses.

I started Walk in the Light Ministries in 1976, and it was incorporated in 1978. In 1980, I went into full-time ministry, meaning I stopped supporting us through other work. We had our first supporters at this time, and we stepped out in faith that God would provide for the needs of Aurica and I, and our nine children.

In 1981, I was invited to a big conference in West Berlin, Germany. I had been called to represent Romania. The conference took place in a huge stadium that held somewhere between eighty and ninety thousand people. I was told that there were at least three thousand Israelites and five thousand Americans in attendance, along with tens of thousands of people from Europe.

This was the first time I ever gathered together with so many wonderful men and women of God. This was where I met Charlie Duke, the astronaut, for the first time. It was here that I heard Charlie Duke's testimony of how he came to the Lord and his experience of walking on the moon. It was also his first experience stepping out into ministry. It was my first journey to give my testimony and to glorify God.

I had preached in many small churches all over, but I had never been in front of such a huge crowd of people representing my country and giving my testimony. Charlie Duke and I became great friends, and we are to this day. Charlie asked me to pray for him, and God gave me some prophetical words and visions for him. Charlie was shocked by this gift that the Lord had bestowed on me.

He was in awe, and said, "How can you tell me exactly what I am thinking and what I am seeking after?"

After a few times of my visions being right, he acknowledged the gifting, drew closer to me, and became a dear friend.

I have had the honor and the privilege of being able to visit him and his family in Texas. I was humbled when he came and visited us in California. Once when we were together, I shared that I had recently gone to Israel. On the return flight, there had been a great storm, and the people on the plane panicked. There were people crying, and many were thinking that it was the end of their lives.

The plane was in terrible turbulence for almost three hours and was almost out of control. I prayed, and God showed me two, huge, giant angels sitting on the wings of the plane.

Just as fear was about to come over me, God spoke to me, "Don't be afraid. My angels will watch over you, and nothing will happen to you." Immediately, I shared with those around me that there was nothing to worry about. Charlie shared the vision with his father one day.

His father said, "Did you ask him if the angels had parachutes? If I ever see angels, they better have parachutes on." I don't know what Charlie told him. I imagine he probably smiled or laughed.

About a year later, Charlie was visiting the area of Orange County, California. He had come for a mayor's prayer breakfast. I had the privilege of picking him up at the airport, taking him to the breakfast meeting, and then back to the airport again. On the way back to the airport, Charlie asked me to pray for his father who was very ill. Charlie was on his way to South Carolina to see him at the hospital.

As Charlie's plane took off, I began to pray and God gave me a vision. I saw an angel with a parachute come and take his father up to heaven. I called Charlie's wife. She was happy to hear about the vision, and she said she would call Charlie. Soon afterwards, God took Charlie's father to heaven. Charlie was disappointed and sad that he hadn't gotten there in time to say good-bye to his father.

Charlie's wife relayed my message about the angels with parachutes and a few days after the funeral we discussed it; neither of us remembering that conversation from a year before. We prayed that God would show us the reason for the parachutes in the vision, and days later, God reminded him of that moment with his father where they had laughed at the thought of angels with parachutes, perched on the wings of a plane. Charlie was comforted as God showed him His unfailing love.

BIBLICAL AND LIFE APPLICATION

Isn't it wonderful that we serve a God who loves us so much that He will go out of his way to show us? The Bible refers to Jesus as the bridegroom. He is the one that will come for His people. This act of unfailing love demonstrates the love of the bridegroom for the bride.

Though he brings grief, he will show compassion, so great is his unfailing love. Lamentations 3:32 NIV

I was overwhelmed with these feelings from the Holy Spirit, and almost as quickly, I was overcome with great weariness. I was so tired that I laid down and slept in the back seat. The next thing I knew, someone was poking me in my ribs or so it seemed. It really felt like someone was trying to wake me by force. As I forced my eyes to focus, I found that I was alone in the van! The people I had been traveling with were nowhere to be seen. The van had stopped, and I didn't know where I was. I had terrible pain in my head and it was heavy. I was finding it almost impossible to hold my head up. I could hear noises outside the vehicle, and I started to pound on the doors and yell for help in German, hoping someone would hear the banging.

Someone came with a tool, like a screwdriver, and forced the door open. I have no idea what I looked like when they opened the door. At some point, I had gotten sick and vomited all over myself. I probably looked like a terrible drunk. Eventually, they got me out of the van; I could hardly stand up. By then, the Austrian police had arrived, and I was told that I was near the Czechoslovakian and Hungarian border, in a small town called Brooke.

The police asked where I was headed, and I told them that I had started out in the direction of Switzerland. They asked what I was doing there, and I said I didn't know. I told them that I had been a passenger, and that evidently the van had broken down because I had seen a large pool of oil under the van when I got out. I told them that something went wrong, and how I had become so sleepy.

After asking me some more questions, I was taken to a clinic where they ran some tests. They were shocked to find that I had many sleeping agents in my system. So many, in fact, that I should have slept for at least forty-eight hours before being aware of my surroundings.

These people had every intention of transporting me across the border and delivering me to Czechoslovakia or Hungary. Both of these countries were under communist control, and I would have been sent on to Romania from there.

A car with diplomatic plates was seen coming into the parking lot. The police realized that it probably had been sent to get me.

These were special cars that had advantages. They were like the secret police or the FBI. They could go anywhere and wouldn't be stopped at the borders.

The Lord had woken me when I was so over-drugged. Tests later revealed that there were so many drugs in my blood stream that I should have slept for at least another twenty-four hours. God surrounded my car with people. He placed tourists there, just at the right moment, who heard my cries for help. He sent the Austrian police just minutes before the arrival of that transport car.

I went to the American embassy in Vienna and told them what had happened. I was told that I was lucky that I hadn't disappeared forever. As that reality sank in, I was overwhelmed with a gripping fear. I suddenly felt that every person who looked at me was after me and had been sent as a spy to find me.

I got on the train and headed to Burne, Switzerland. There my friends were waiting in a state of despair. They knew I was overdue and missing, and they didn't know where to begin to look for me.

When I arrived and explained what had happened and described the fear that was binding me, they prayed for me, and I was immediately released from it.

(Ilie broke out in praise at this point. "Praise the Lord! I was able to be free again. I give all the glory to God because He protects me!")

BIBLICAL AND LIFE APPLICATION

This experience was one of the most interesting that I've had. We always have to pray and wait for the Lord to receive His confirmation. We can make mistakes if we pray and then make decisions too quickly. Many times, I've had to experience difficult tests. Sometimes I went through difficult times because I prayed brief prayers. Then I wouldn't wait long enough on the Lord before making a decision. It is important to be patient and wait for the answer. Patience and hope work together. They guide and lead us toward the blessings of the Lord so that we can inherit all the blessings of the Lord.

Not only so, but we also rejoice in our sufferings, because we know that suffering produces perseverance; perseverance, character; and character, hope. And hope does not disappoint us, because God has poured out His love into our hearts by the Holy Spirit, whom he has given us. Romans 5:3-5 NIV

We can learn from this experience. When Satan wants to open a false door and confuse us or open the wrong way before us, he can cause us to try to think that there is some big advantage. He confuses us. The enemy sometimes makes us believe that everything is going to be better or for our good.

For though we live in the world, we do not wage war as the world does. The weapons we fight with are not the weapons of the world. On the contrary, they have divine power to demolish strongholds. We demolish arguments and every pretension that sets itself up against the knowledge of God, and we take captive every thought to make it obedient to Christ.
2 Corinthians 10:3-5 NIV

THE TOUCH OF
THE MASTER'S HAND

Another incident from 1983 had to do with my son, Benjamin. Benjamin was special as a child, having many medical difficulties. This was due in part to the medical treatments Aurica underwent in Austria for tuberculosis. She had undergone treatments for a total of six months, and her body needed time to rid itself of the medication.

Soon after Aurica came to America, we found that we were expecting. In nine months Benjamin was born. This was too soon for her body to have completely flushed the medications from her lung treatments, and the medicine affected the development of our new baby. Benny never developed like the other children. Over the years, many doctors from Hollywood and Los Angeles saw Benny. They said he would never speak or walk and that his life would be spent in a wheelchair. I don't know the correct medical term, but they would say that because of the way his bones were structured they would never be strong enough for him to stand and walk.

At age two, when the other children had already taken to walking, Benny was just learning to crawl. One day, and I don't know how old he was when this happened, Benny was crawling outside while the other children were playing near the pool. Suddenly, Benny pulled himself up and started walking! It was, at once, interesting and curious since we had been told there was no hope. Benny walked from that day forward.

My wife and I decided to stop taking him to doctors since it seemed more like torture than treatment. He would spend whole days in hospitals undergoing all kinds of examinations. We just determined to let God decide what was best for Benny. After Benny had been walking for some time, I took him to see a Romanian-Jewish doctor, Dr. Meyers, in Los Angles for a check up. She couldn't believe it was Benny.

Dr. Meyers said, "This can't be Benny. This is Johnny."

God had worked a miracle and was healing Benny. In 1983, we moved to New Cuyama, California, so I could work on a farm. We lived there for almost six months. The children loved it. There was plenty of room to run and roam, and lots of nature and wildlife to watch, including snakes and rabbits.

When Benny was around six and Johnny was five, they caught a big snake and put him in a box. One of their older brothers recognized it as a poisonous snake. Here were those kids playing with a very large, very dangerous snake, but God had protected them and kept them from harm!

All day long the children would chase all kinds of creatures. The farm was over two thousand acres and was home to a private airstrip; there was plenty of room to explore. The older boys, Dan and Sam, became avid hunters of rabbits. They brought home plenty of bounty until I begged them to stop. We had too much to use already.

One day the keys were left in the ignition of an old pickup truck. The older boys had used it to go hunting. They had run home to clean up and change for church. As we were all piling into the van and finding a seat, we lost track of Benny and Johnny. Benny had paused to play with the tricycle in the driveway, and Johnny, our little fiery child, had climbed into the truck next to the van.

We all watched in horror—slow motion horror—as Johnny started the truck. It was a stick shift and had been left in gear. As the truck started, it shot forward landing on top of Benny. It had happened so quickly, right in front of us, yet we had been powerless to do anything to prevent it from happening.

We all jumped out of the van, and Dan and I tried to pick up the truck. The wheel was directly on top of Benny's head. As we lifted, I was struck by severe pain in my back, and I fell down and couldn't stand. When Benny was finally pulled out, I couldn't believe my eyes. Benny's head looked like a flat tire. He wasn't crying, but his eyes were bulging and full of blood. There was blood coming through the pores of his face. By now neighbors had heard our cries, and someone had called an ambulance.

Benny was rushed to the hospital in town, but they weren't equipped to handle such trauma. Benny was sent to another larger hospital nearby. Miraculously, Benny was still alive, though no doctor could understand why. Benny was immediately hooked up to all kinds of machines. He was X-rayed and put on oxygen. Aurica and I weren't allowed to see him.

After three hours a nurse came out and said, "It's incredible. His head is back to normal!"

A few hours after that, they allowed us to go in and see Benny. Benny started to cry when he saw us. The doctors said it was amazing. There was no explanation for his recovery. The bones in his skull should have been crushed. The doctors suggested that we take the story to the television show, 20-20, so that the rest of the nation could hear what had happened. Within a few days, after they had observed him for a while, we took Benny home again completely restored and fully healed. Praise the Lord!

Today, Benny is an active, walking, talking adult. Benny joins in and maintains conversations with ease. He has a bit of a nasal twang in his voice. He drives big rig trucks and is very much aware of God's hand on his life.

BIBLICAL AND LIFE APPLICATION

God is a miracle working God. His love for us extends farther than we can begin to imagine. His healing power is more than we can dare to dream of. The nurse called this "incredible" and the doctors called it "amazing." There is only one word to describe such an event—MIRACULOUS.

He performs wonders that cannot be fathomed,
miracles that cannot be counted.
Job 5:9 NIV

Just two months after Iliuta died, I nearly lost Johnny. I had asked Lidia and Marianna to watch Johnny while I put Benjamin down for a nap. Little Benny had many medical problems, so I always had to take plenty of time to work with him and settle him into his naps.

Johnny, bless him, was a little ball of energy that could get into more trouble than I care to remember. On this occasion, he somehow managed to get the gate to the pool unlocked and got into or fell into the pool. I was coming down the hall and saw something floating in the pool! My stomach dropped, and I knew, just knew, it was Johnny.

I was running and shouting, "Johnny is drowning! Where are you girls?"

Fivi was just coming in the front door from school and heard me shouting. She ran straight through the house, dove into the pool, and brought Johnny to the side. When we pulled him out, he was purple. We were praying and crying out to God as we laid him on the ground. We watched in breathless wonder as the water just drained out of him—just like it had with his father so many years before. He started crying, and I called for an ambulance. He was checked out and pronounced to be fine. Johnny was still a spitfire that got into every kind of trouble, but he did gain a new respect for water that day.

Another problem that surfaced in the coming months and years was rebellion in Daniel. Dan was very angry with God over Iliuta, and he started running away. He would come back and be obedient and wonderful for a time. Then he would slack off, become rebellious, and run away again.

I won't go into all the details here, but I will say that through it all, God kept His hand upon Daniel. Proverbs 22:6 says, *"Train up a child in the way he should go and when he is old he will not depart from it."* I can testify that this scripture is true.

We had many problems with Daniel, but we never stopped

praying for him. In fact, he will be the first to tell you that prayer was a turning point for him. Once when he was out, he had a strong urge to return home. When he was a block away from the house, he heard a loud voice talking. As he approached the house, he realized we were praying. He could hear us through the open window.

We were praying, "Dear Lord, bring Daniel home."

We had no idea where he was or if he was safe. He'd been gone for weeks. God orchestrated the timing of his return so he would hear and see his father and I on our knees praying for him. It struck his heart and was the moment when he started turning his life around and coming back to the Lord.

Today Daniel is a pastor and the Ministry Director for Walk in the Light. He works out of the office in Washington, Missouri. Previously, he served in Romania, pastoring the church in Raduati, for ten years before coming to the States. He has a lovely wife and five beautiful children. Daniel is very open about his testimony, so I'll let him tell his own story.

TRAGEDY BECOMES A MIRACLE

Four years after little Iliuta died, my wife and I were traveling with our four youngest children in Maryland and Virginia. I was on a mission trip and had been blessed to appear on the 700 Club to give my testimony. We had decided to stop in Baltimore and visit with our dear friends, Pastor Dick Royer and his wife, Sister Sue.

The following day was beautiful, and we all went to a local park before beginning our return drive to California. The park was known for its lovely grounds, and we wanted to take some pictures while we were there. Aurica and I, our children, and Sister Sue all sat scrunched together on a bench, and Pastor Dick took a picture. Then he and I switched places, and another picture was taken.

The rest of our time was uneventful, and we began our trek back to California. I didn't think much about those pictures. We took them in to be developed and picked them up several days later when Dan and I were on our way out of town. We were en route to Texas for another mission trip. I paid for the pictures, and as I was driving out of town, Dan began to look through the photos that had been taken.

All of a sudden, Dan became excited and asked me, "Dad, what is with this picture? What happened with this picture? Look, can you see Iliuta in this picture?"

It had been four years since Iliuta had died. Dan was so shaken by what he was seeing that I pulled the car off the road so I could see too. There in the picture, right before my eyes, was the photo that Pastor Dick had taken at the park. Iliuta was standing behind Aurica and me. He was dressed in his little outfit and smiling into the camera. He wasn't as defined as the rest of us, yet I instantly knew who he was. Curiously, there was also another little girl in the picture that I didn't recognize.

Everyone who saw the picture and had known Iliuta recognized him immediately. The picture was analyzed by the 700 Club and declared to be authentic. It was a real photo that had not been tampered with and one of only a few like it. Daniel was greatly influenced and touched by the way God works and how He took Iliuta home to be with Him. Many other young people were also touched and affected by the photo and the testimony of it.

Shortly after the photo was discovered, I was in an airport in Dallas waiting for some other brothers in the Lord to arrive from different states. We were going to travel on together to another pastor's conference. As I was waiting, I got into a conversation with some of the ladies sitting around me. I began to witness and share about the Lord.

They noticed my accent and broken English, and one lady wanted to know where I was from. I told her that I was from Romania. One of the ladies looked at me and tears began to fill her eyes. I entered into a deeper discussion with her. I discovered that her daughter-in-law had been through a very difficult time after being in an accident in Garden Grove, California. She had accidentally struck and killed a small Romanian boy.

The lady told me that after the accident, her daughter-in-law had been struck by fear, and for days, she would not leave the house. By chance, one day she turned on the television and found an evangelist preaching.

The evangelist said, "The devil wants to bring condemnation on someone. The devil wants to put someone in a prison of condemnation, but God wants to bring deliverance."

At that moment, she asked Jesus to come into her heart, and then she shared with everyone what had happened. Her mother-in-law, the lady I was speaking with, also accepted Christ that day, as well as several other family members.

By this time, I was weeping with joy, and she asked why I was crying. I told her that the little boy her daughter-in-law had killed was my own son, Iliuta. Then we were crying together.

BIBLICAL AND LIFE APPLICATION

At Iliuta's funeral, Pastor Paul had preached from Romans 8:28. God works all things together for the good for those who love Him. Even through hard and difficult times, He does His work. Victory belongs to the Lord. Our biggest challenge is releasing our pain, anger, and hurt back to Him, so He can then use it for His glory.

*And we know that in all things God works for the good of those who love him, who have been called according to his purpose. For those God foreknew he also predestined to be conformed to the likeness of his Son...*Romans 8:28-29a NIV

What, then, shall we say in response to this? If God is for us, who can be against us? Romans 8:31 NIV

When we give Jesus our broken lives, broken dreams, and broken hearts, He takes the shattered pieces and uses them to reach the hurting and lost. Only someone who has lost a child can truly understand that pain. Only someone who has been abandoned, divorced, or abused can understand the suffering of another person in similar circumstances. When we release these areas of our lives back to Him, God uses us in our weaknesses. Our sacrifice feeds a multitude.

Taking the five loaves and the two fish and looking up to heaven, he gave thanks and broke the loaves. Then he gave them to his disciples to set before the people. He also divided the two fish among them all. Mark 6:41 NIV

"GO TO WASHINGTON"

We all liked California, and I thought we would always live there. Eventually, the Lord convinced us that He wanted us to move. The problem was, we didn't know where we were supposed to move. In prayer, God said we would move to Washington. At first, I thought God meant the state of Washington since I had visited there and liked it very much. Then I thought maybe He had meant Washington D.C. since we had friends there.

In 1985, we put our house on the market. We tried to sell it through a couple of real estate agents, but it would not sell. However, when the Lord prepares, He prepares everything. The Lord had spoken to us that we would be moving to Washington. We both had a dream, my wife and I, and we each saw a beautiful white house sitting on a hill with lots of land around it. When we woke up, we both knew this was our house.

Again, we put our house on the market. Only this time we didn't use a Realtor. We then left on a mission trip around the United States. One of our stops was in Texas, where we visited with one of our good friends, Brother Robert Ewing. Brother Robert wanted us to move there, and we saw that living there would work well for us. We prayed and debated the pros and the cons. We nearly decided to move there, yet something, some small voice, kept prodding us to continue our search.

From there, we went to Little Rock, Arkansas, where we have many other friends and saw many beautiful places. It seemed very open for us to move there as well, but the unsettled feeling remained. So our search continued. From Little Rock, we traveled on towards Virginia and the Washington D.C. area.

In Washington D.C., we saw many friends, and we even looked at houses that were for sale. However, we didn't have peace about any of them, and things didn't seem clear. From there, we traveled to Goshen, Indiana, where we also looked at some houses. We saw a house that looked similar to the one we had seen in our dreams, but we both felt that the house in the dream had been empty.

From Goshen, we drove to DuQuoin, Illinois, where we found a beautiful white house, but it was not for sale. Our good friend, Pastor Percy Pavlof, lived in that area, and he encouraged us to live there. However, we knew it was not the place for us, so on we went. Our next stop was in St. Clair, Missouri. There we visited Bob and Sylvia Pellen. We stayed with them a few days and asked if they knew of any houses for sale.

They put us in touch with a Realtor in the area who could show us some houses. When we met with the Realtor, I shared with her the dream of the house that God had waiting for us. I described it to her.

As I was sharing she began to smile, "Oh, I know the house. In Washington, I have a house that is similar to what you are describing."

When we got to the house, Aurica and I felt like it was the one from our dream. This was the home for us. We made an offer and left to go back to California. Our offer was twenty thousand dollars less than what they were asking for. Our offer was rejected. When we got back to California, we had an offer on our house, and it was sold. We made another offer on the house in Washington, Missouri. They accepted the price we offered but not the move-in date. They wanted to wait until after we had closed on the loan. I applied for the bank loan but was turned down because I only had a small salary at the time.

Now we had no home. We packed up and moved with the children across the country and stayed with our friends, Bob and Sylvia Pellen, for a time. We looked for a house to rent, and eventually, we found an old house. It was one hundred forty years old with one bathroom. It was in Washington, near the bank and across the street from the high school. The house has since been torn down, and they have built a small nursing home on the site.

We were living in this old house with one bathroom and eight children. Fivi was married by this time. In addition to the ten of us, my mother was visiting from Romania. After she left, another Romanian friend, Jacob, moved in with his flock of children—all twelve of them. No one wanted to rent to him with twelve children.

So here we were. Had we heard wrong? In California, we had a house with six bedrooms, three bathrooms, a big yard, and a swimming pool. Now we were living with twenty-one children and four adults sharing one bathroom. The time spent each morning waiting in line to use the bathroom, as everyone got ready for school, was unbelievable.

I started questioning that I had heard God correctly. The children were murmuring and complaining. The house God had set aside for us was empty, yet the bank rejected our loan request. The more we tried to rush, the more barricades seemed to come against us.

I finally applied with a different bank and was approved for a loan. We were able to buy the house on South Point Road. It is the one we own to this very day.

BIBLICAL AND LIFE APPLICATION

There are many trials on the road to God's blessings. Sometimes we have to be patient a long time. Everything God begins in our life, He will bring to completion as long as we trust Him.

God uses timing as a way to refine us and prepare us for the next phase of our journey. God knows there are many things in us that need to be refined. One of the biggest challenges we face is not becoming frustrated while we wait. We cannot rush His timing or murmur. Murmuring can also be called complaining. Who are we to complain about anything that God does? We only run the risk of more problems or further delays with murmuring!

Now the people complained about their hardships in the hearing of the Lord, and when he heard them his anger was aroused. Numbers 11:1 NIV

WITH HEALING IN
HIS WINGS

For many years, I had battled against Satan in regard to a healing that the Lord had done in my body. It was not a healing that had come all at once. It was a healing that had come over time. Many doctors had told me that I needed to have an operation on my back to repair three damaged vertebrae. These vertebrae were threatening to cripple me or make me permanently hunched over.

Over time, God set me free from the pain that I felt. The devil, of course, was always there to tell me that I had lived with this for twenty-five years and wasn't really healed. He tried to get me to believe that having this pain for twenty-five years meant that I would always have the pain.

God spoke to me at one point and said, "Trust me and speak the words, 'I am healed.'"

So every time those thoughts entered my mind I would state, "In the name of Jesus, I am healed. I am healed."

By repeating those words over and over, I eventually realized that I was, in fact, healed. Unlike most healings, I cannot tell you the day and hour that it happened. I just knew to trust Him to meet my need. To this day, I have a strong healthy back.

In 1988, I returned from another mission trip. I wasn't feeling well, but it wasn't my back that was bothering me. I went to my friend, Dr. Lou, in Orange County, California, upon my return. After running many tests, he discovered that I had an enlarged heart. According to Dr. Lou, I either needed an operation very soon, or I needed a miracle.

This was during the time that many false rumors were circulating that the Lord would return on a certain date. I was very weak and had very little strength or stamina. I returned to Washington, Missouri, to rest and recuperate from my trip.

I was lying down one day when there was a sudden wind in

the room. I looked at the windows thinking they were open, but they were, in fact, shut. It seemed to me that the house and bed was shaking, and in an instant, there at the foot of the bed, I saw a vision of a giant eagle standing and looking at me. The eagle stretched out his wing and touched my chest.

At that moment, I went into a trance or was unconscious. I was like this for a time, and when I came to, I could feel heat on my chest where the wing had touched me. I wasn't sure what had happened, but I felt better and stronger. I sat up and looked down to see a white line on my chest. It was approximately 10-12 inches in length and about as thick as my finger.

I showed my wife, my children, and my pastor the line on my chest. From that day on, I felt wonderful. It was as if God had performed an operation on me, healing me of an enlarged heart. The white line was just for my benefit so that I could see the evidence of healing.

I believe God performed this operation on me. It seemed so big to us, but for God, it was a simple thing. Shortly after this happened, I traveled to Japan and set up an office there. From that time, I have been strengthened and have been able to travel the world.

(Brother Ilie burst out with, "Glory to God! The Lord is good! Hallelujah!")

But for you who revere my name, the sun of righteousness will rise with healing in its wings. Malachi 4:2 NIV

FROM MAN'S JAILHOUSE TO GOD'S STOREHOUSE

Despite my joy of living in America and the work that the Lord had given me to do, I still had frustration in my heart. Life in Romania, which had been good, was deteriorating rapidly. The little information that we got from family and friends still inside the country related stories of hopelessness and despair. Long lines and empty stores confirmed the poverty felt by all. The government, which had once boasted to all that they would lead easy, good lives, now spent all its time controlling the rebellion that was simmering under the surface.

I felt helpless, unable to do anything more than continue to sponsor as many families into America as possible. In addition, Aurica and I spent many hours on our knees praying for our homeland. In my heart I longed to do more.

Six months before the borders to Romania opened to the world, I was in Germany preaching. I had a vision one night. In this vision, a man came towards me from a desert-like area. He was wearing dark brown, striped clothing that reminded me of prison clothing. He asked me what he could do because of all the trouble in Romania. I was impressed with three things, and in the vision, I told him what needed to happen in Romania:

1. The Romanian people needed to recognize Jesus in their hearts as Savior and Lord.

2. The Romanian people needed the freedom found in Christ.

3. The government needed to give the people's land back because the earth belongs to the Lord.

In the vision, the man turned around and walked back into the desert. He walked until I could no longer see him. After the vision ended, I was impressed in my spirit that the man was Ceausescu. I was sharing this vision six months before the borders opened. There were many people praying and fasting for a change in government and for the freedom of Berlin. The wall in Berlin fell in 1989, and the revolution started in Timisoara, Romania, at nearly the same time, on December 12, 1989.

At this time, I was at home in Missouri and had no idea what was happening. I was in prayer, and one night, I had a dream in which night was transformed into day in an instant. God spoke to me and said that everything was going to change. Everything would be exposed to the light. Everything would be clarified, and everything that had been working in hiding would be exposed to the light. While I was still sorting out what I had seen and heard, the phone rang, and it was Pastor Tingi Kimura from Tokyo, Japan.

Pastor Tingi was excited and wanted to know if I knew what was happening in Romania. I said, "No," and he told me to go turn on the television immediately. I couldn't believe what I was seeing. I was watching the revolution unfold before my eyes in my own living room. I realized, in my dream, God had been telling me that the days of communism were about to end. In the end, God had the victory, and He brought to light all the atrocities that had gone on while the rest of the world went about its business.

As I watched, God gave me the desire to return to Romania and a vision for what needed to be done there. I flew to Switzerland and spoke to my brothers in area churches. Many from Austria, Germany, and Switzerland joined me. We had no idea how we would do it as we had no cars or trucks. Suddenly, we had eight vehicles, and we filled them with food, clothing, medical aid, supplies, and Bibles. For the first time in sixteen years, I reentered the country.

It was a miracle how God pulled it all together—all the supplies, thirty people, and vehicles in two weeks! I had left Romania running for my life with only two men, and now I was returning with an army of thirty, carrying Bibles—the very reason we had had to flee! What a contrast! Only God could arrange such a feat!

The prison in which I had been jailed, interrogated, and beaten so many times was now used to house the truckloads of Bibles we brought. I cried with joy in my heart at this image.

I worshipped the Lord there saying, "Lord, You are so great and wonderful! You can change all things."

So God brought His light to Romania. He overturned the power of communism and darkness, and He brought the light of the Gospel and freedom to a dying nation.

BIBLICAL AND LIFE APPLICATION

So often situations that have remained in a locked and mired state will collapse, seemingly overnight. God knows the day and hour of everything that He plans to do. Nothing will be overlooked. Nothing will be early, and nothing will be late. Everything will be completed in His perfect timing, according to His perfect plan. When we truly grasp this as fact and allow the knowledge of it to sink into our minds and spirits, we can take comfort.

The walls of Jericho collapsed after the people shouted and blew the trumpets, but for seven days, they had marched around the city in preparation for that moment. God destroyed the wall in His timing, but the people were first obedient in faith. We must always do our part in prayer and faith, and trust God to bring change in His timing.

When the trumpets sounded, the people shouted, and at the sound of the trumpet, when the people gave a loud shout, the wall collapsed; so every man charged straight in, and they took the city. Joshua 6:20 NIV

When the government collapsed, we were there charging back into the cities with all the supplies we could get our hands on. How awesome of God to take the jail, used to abuse so many people for so long, and turn it into a storehouse for His glory! God never ceases to amaze me!

The Lord said, "I have indeed seen the misery of my people in Egypt. I have heard them crying out because of their slave drivers, and I am concerned about their suffering. So I have come down to rescue them from the hand of the Egyptians..." Exodus 3:7-8a NIV

Ilie watched the unfolding collapse of the communist government in Romania on television. The phone was ringing constantly. Friends from all over the world were calling to see if he was watching the news. The chaos of revolution started in mid-December 1989. That was the part we all saw on television, but it actually started before that with a Hungarian reform priest named Laslo. He spoke out against what was happening in Romania. The secret police came to arrest him, but were met by his congregation. More police arrived, and more citizens came to his aid. Even more police arrived, and even more citizens came to his aid. It was God's timing. One small voice started a tidal wave that swept across the nation.

Another area where the rebellion began with a strong stand was at the colleges. At this point, the young people were so poor and had no hope for the future. Most struggled to find and pay for the basics like food and heat.

When the army realized that the secret police were killing their own [the army's] family members, the government factions started fighting from within. The army, in turn, came against the secret police.

Behind all of this were years of prayers and tears to God for deliverance. Ilie and I had been praying for Romania for as long as we could remember. Many thousands of people and their prayers had gone before us to lay the groundwork for the sudden collapse of communism.

When Ceausescu was killed on December 25, 1989, the grip was finally broken. As Ilie watched the miracle unfolding on television, he was on the phone with Rolf Buerki in Switzerland. Together, they began to plan a trip with humanitarian aid back into the country. Within two weeks, they had organized a team of thirty people, an 18-wheeler loaded with fifteen thousand Bibles, food, medical supplies, and other humanitarian aid. In addition, there were ten to fifteen vans loaded with more of the same.

We flew into Switzerland and then went on to Vienna where we had a small apartment. We stayed there the first night, then left Vienna at seven in the evening, and drove all night. We encountered bad weather with lots of snow and arrived at the Romanian border at seven the next morning. In my heart, I was very nervous. What would happen? Was Romania really free? Would they let us in? Would there be trouble? But as we came close to the border gates, there was a huge sign that said "WELCOME TO FREE ROMANIA!"

The border had guards and civilians mixing together, and we were greeted with much joy. They asked for Bibles, and we freely passed them out. We took pictures with them, and they asked for Bibles for their family members. So we handed out more Bibles. We witnessed everywhere we went, and the people were open and received Jesus.

The people would say, "Come. Now we receive you. The devil has taken Ceausescu."

We arrived at Bistrita about three or four in the afternoon. We stopped for the night at a hotel called Coroana de Aur, which means "Crown of Gold." Ilie witnessed to everyone at the hotel and gave each hotel worker a Bible. People heard we had arrived, and an impromptu evangelistic meeting was held in front of the police station.

The next day, we drove north for 250 kilometers. The road was so rough, it took eight hours to arrive at our next destination. The road was riddled with potholes, mountain passes, and dangerous curves. Where possible, people would line the sides of the roads and wave to us. We, in turn, would throw candy to the children along the route. Finally, we reached the town of Dornesti and unloaded the truck at the little church there. The mayor and chief of police came and organized the locals to help unload the truck.

We handed out supplies to everyone. We almost had a riot as people rushed us, desperate for supplies. The people were so poor and hungry. As far as the eye could see, they were coming. Many people received goods, handed items off to their children, and then got back into the throng to get more. They were afraid that freedom might not last very long. Some people used extra supplies to sell to others as a way to gain some income.

We gave away sugar, flour, and rice. Up to this point, these had been rationed items, and a family of five would only receive two kilograms per month. Single adults would only receive one half of a kilogram per month. A family of three received only one kilogram per month. People would stand in line all day to receive these rations. No wonder they were so hungry!

Daniel still remembers one old man who came to the relief station. He was crying, and he didn't ask for any food or other supplies; he only wanted a Bible. The man kissed Daniel's sister, Lidia, on the hand, knelt in the dirt, and asked for a Bible. It was a humbling experience for us all.

At that time, you could share the Gospel for just a few minutes and fifty people or more would accept Jesus. It was the same everywhere we went. We rented the biggest hall, the movie theatre, on a Saturday and held an old-fashioned tent meeting. It was standing room only that day. The theatre had never had so many patrons! We preached and shared. So many gave their hearts to the Lord that day.

On the streets, we could see so many poor children begging. These children had been abandoned. Their parents had died or been killed by the regime and begging was their only way to survive.

We visited the state-run orphanage, and the conditions there were horrible. The children had lice and other conditions. The babies were left in cribs alone in dark, dingy rooms all day and night without love and hope. It was more than I could bear to see.

The Lord planted in Ilie's heart to build an orphanage. However, we only had three or four supporters who helped to bring families into America. Ilie traveled to Japan on a preaching engagement and shared the vision the Lord had given him.   The Holy Spirit touched one man, and he donated twenty thousand dollars in cash. He was the first to donate to help the project. Daniel went with his father on that trip and said repeatedly that he has never seen so much money. In 1991, twenty thousand dollars went a long way.

We built the first building with that donation. When partially complete, we moved in seven children and fourteen workers. By the time the building was completely finished and stocked, we probably spent around fifty thousand dollars. Today that one building is worth over half a million U.S. dollars.

Even before receiving that first donation, we began to do the work that God had given us. Almost immediately after receiving the vision, we rented a small house by faith and took in those first seven children and fourteen workers. We housed the children there until the orphanage was built. The house was in Radauti, and we had some volunteer workers from America early on. Nancy was one of our first volunteer nurses, and she still works with the ministry today.

The faithful people in Japan sent a prayer team early on, and they were with us for several weeks. Their entire job at the ministry during that season was prayer. They prayed for eight hours every day, stopping only for a lunch break. It was an important groundbreaking time for the ministry, and they provided needed prayer cover. The enemy tried many things to destroy the work, including a fire at the storage shed that has never been explained. Another time, the septic tank was giving us problems. We had never seen a septic company at work anywhere. Daniel drove towards town hoping to find someone who would know where to locate such a company. Along the way, he passed a septic repair truck, and the man agreed to come and work on the septic for us. God knew our needs and sent the truck to us!

That year, we held the first daytime legal baptism, and a church in Bistrita organized it. Over one hundred fifty people came to be baptized that first year. There were five thousand family and friends to watch and celebrate with them. We marched through the streets like a parade with a band, and we all sang songs and stopped periodically to recite poems about the Lord and His goodness.

The people would shout, "Glory! Glory! Hallelujah! We are free now!" Christians were no longer afraid to live their lives and to glorify God.

That first baptism, celebrated in freedom, was such a stark contrast to the last one that we held before Ilie fled the country. What was done in the depths of darkness and secrecy was now celebrated openly at the height of day and with a parade. What an awesome God we serve!

WITHOUT A VISION THE PEOPLE PERISH

In 1990, we rented a big house, and we took in seven children in Raduati. Eventually, we had twenty children that we cared for. In 1991, we started construction of the first children's home.

I didn't have any idea how we could make it happen, but God had said, "By faith do everything I tell you, and in the right time, I will provide everything you need. You have to take a step of faith every day, and I will help you."

God gave me a vision of how the building should be built. He showed me how it should have two levels, how the windows should be built, and how a dove should be placed on the peak of the roof pointing west towards America. We dedicated that building on October 17, 1992, the same weekend as my son's wedding, and we moved in with all the children. The building wasn't completely done. We completed construction the following year.

In 1995, the Lord instructed me to go west about two hundred fifty to three hundred kilometers from where we had built the first orphanage. There I found a piece of land that Ceausescu had wanted to build a hunting lodge on. He had visited there about a month before he was executed by a firing squad. We were put in touch with some people who were high up in the government, and we were given the land.

I was still saying, "Lord what will we do here? There is no road, no water, no electricity, and no phones." We now had hectares (acres) of land in the middle of nowhere.

Just like before, we started everything by faith. Within a few short years, we had several houses and a working farm. As of October 2004, we house over 50 toddlers and six teenagers at Livezile. At Dornesti, we currently house 38 children. In total, we have around one hundred employees working at Dornesti, Livezile, and the farm.

We help many other families with children in both areas. If you added up all the children that are in family units that we have helped and supported, they would add up to approximately five hundred children. This is in addition to the children that we house and feed daily. By helping these families, we are keeping their family units intact. Parents are not forced to make agonizing decisions; whether to keep their children and watch them starve or give them away and know they have food and shelter. We are supporting them through different programs that we have. We also have some children in foster care that we are helping to support.

We believe the work God has given us will go forward. God gave us a vision for a church in Raduati, which we were able to build. We give all the glory to God for its existence. He provided it, and we have no debt. For seven years, we moved from place to place renting and holding church. Sometimes we couldn't find a place to rent. After seven years of praying together as a church, we were able to build, and Daniel pastored there. We established a Bible School and a Training Center to raise up disciples. Many lives have been touched. Many people are coming to the Lord, being baptized, and discipled. The children are coming to church, and the church is growing.

In 2001, the Lord opened the door to go on television in Romania. All the people were blessed and happy to see the work of the Lord. Many people came a great distance to see for themselves that we were really there. They wanted to make sure that what they had seen on the television was true. For the first time, I was able to pray for the deliverance of the people on national television. I was able to witness about the power of deliverance and the healing power of Jesus Christ.

The people are so hungry for the Word and are seeking the Lord. In the beginning we were so flooded with phone calls and letters requesting Bibles, that I had to hire someone to answer the phone, answer letters, and send Bibles across the nation. God has opened a great door of opportunity on radio and television in Romania to share the gospel. At this time, four major national channels and one regional channel are allowing us to share and preach on a regular basis.

God has helped us to bring a living testimony to the people, so they can see the fruit of this work. They come great distances to see what we are doing. They help us in any way they can through work, finance, or prayer. Many people have offered to donate land so that we can build in other areas. Others want to donate buildings for our use.

At this point, we cannot branch out further in any other areas. First, we are waiting for the work in Livezile to be brought to completion. Then we will see where the Lord will send us next.

In the state-run orphanages, the children have to leave at eighteen. We want a place where the children can grow and have a place to live as long as they want. We never force them to leave simply because they have reached a certain age. Many of the children choose to stay with us and, in turn, become involved in the work of the Lord, helping the younger children coming in. Others have chosen to go out into the world, to marry, and work elsewhere. A few have gone on to college to pursue larger endeavors. We rejoice with each one.

In the near future, we hope to have a grade school, later a high school, and a Bible college for those who are called to serve. We also desire to do something for the elderly because it seems like no one is paying any attention to them and their needs. Many feel forsaken, forgotten, and cast away. This is our vision for the future: to expand and develop places of work for the children in a Christian community, schooling, and a place of care for the elderly.

As Romania continues the process of joining the European Union, new challenges continue to arise. We face seemingly insurmountable obstacles in paperwork and red tape, mandatory wage increases, adoption holds, changes in building codes, and the like. But we rest, knowing that our loving Father watches over all.

God bless you all,

Brother Ilie

Walk in the Light Ministries was originally founded to bring relief to Romanian refugees around the world. In 1989, its focus shifted to providing shelter and hope to Romania's orphaned and abandoned children. The first orphanage was established in Dornesti in 1991. It housed and cared for 14 children in the first year.

Walk in the Light Ministries founded a second location called The Children's Village at Livezile in 1995, which currently houses over 50 infants, toddlers, and teens.

Over the years, several hundred children have been housed, cared for, and shown the love of Christ at Dornesti and Livezile.

Our on-going mission is to provide safe housing for these children, good food and clothing, adequate medical care, and spiritual guidance.

We care for children of all ages from infancy through the teen years. Many of our teens decide to remain with us as staff members to help provide new children with the same chance at life that they have received.

Now that you've read the stories, we hope you will take the time to learn a little more about our on-going mission.

The Orphanage at Dornesti

Our original complex, Dornesti, opened in 1991, and as of this writing, houses 38 children between the ages of 6 and 18. The children enjoy blessings that most Romanian children don't have.

Not only are they being raised in a Christian atmosphere and being trained in the Word of God, but they are offered more educational opportunities as well. Many of our children did not have an opportunity to attend school on a regular basis before coming to us. They are now tutored daily so they can experience success in the classroom.

The orphanage is near the church established by WITL in the town of Radauti. The Dornesti children enjoy a vibrant church life, receiving and participating in its ministry to the community.

The Dornesti facility is built similar to a college dorm with all children housed under one roof. They sleep two to three children to a room, and there is a kitchen, dining room, and general meeting area, all on the main level.

As you can imagine, there is much noise, laughter, and general chaos with so many children under one roof! They keep the

staff working hard at all times. Mountains of laundry must be done each day, sorted, and returned to each child. Think of it!

Cooking requires much the same challenge. Three meals per day for each hungry, growing child, plus two meals per day for each worker, multiplied by 365 days per year is over 62,000 meals per year!

With each challenge there is much wondrous pleasure, and we invite you to share the experience with us as a short-term mission worker at anytime. The smiles of the children are a reward of their own!

Some of Our Children

The Children's Village at Livezile

The Village consists of four houses, currently housing approximately 50 children, ranging from infant to teen. The actual number of children housed here is changing on

a daily basis because of changing regulations and guidelines in response to joining the European Union.

The first building was opened in 1995 and lies just outside the town of Bistrita in the Transylvania area of Romania.

The village was set up in house-style so that there would be a more home-like atmosphere.

The Farm at Livezile

In order to ensure the best possible nutrition for the children, WITL has begun a working farm at Livezile. It provides food for our children, and we help support many of the area's struggling families with food as well. In addition, our children are gaining valuable life skills to help them in the future. Many of the area adults work at our facility, thus gaining needed income for their families.

We grow potatoes, corn, beets, peas, beans, tomatoes, cabbage, cucumbers, spinach, peppers, and spices. Produce is either eaten fresh or canned for later use.

The Greenhouse at Livezile

The greenhouse is truly a blessing for us. With the cold winters we have in Romania we are able to begin our sprouts earlier and lengthen the growing season, thus providing much needed produce for our facility.

We can grow virtually all our plants in the greenhouse to start, and then transfer them outside after it is warm enough. In addition, we can grow some things even in the winter months.

Irrigation is the biggest challenge. Watering is done by hand because there is no sprinkler system.

Radauti Christian Center

Soon after the establishment of our first orphanage in Dornesti the need for a stable New Testament church in the lives of our children, staff, and missionaries became very evident. Starting in

local homes as a house group, our church grew to include people in the village of Dornesti and the nearby town of Radauti. As the church grew, the meetings moved from place to place (including an old cinema and a bowling alley).

Finally in 1998, the church was able to purchase some land and began construction on a building of their own. Today, the

Radauti Christian Center has a vibrant ministry not only to the orphans and staff at the Dornesti orphanage but the surrounding community as well.

CHURCH LEADERSHIP

The outreaches of the church include a ministry to the poor, a Bible school, and youth and children's ministries. Recently, many of our children had the opportunity to travel to Germany to sing in area churches there and minister the Gospel to others. It was the first time any of them had traveled beyond their village, and it was a great experience for them. This trip was made possible by the donations of our supporters. Recently, we were blessed with a bus so that the children may be transported to other locations for other ministry opportunities and activities.

When we first arrived in Romania, we spent our time handing out Bibles and food to everyone we met. Hundreds flocked to meetings we held in various locations around the city.

YOUTH SINGING GROUP

Here are some of the pictures from those early days. You can see the hopelessness on their faces. That look, the emptiness of

their eyes, and lack of expression are the images that are ever before us as we press on in His service.

People gathered quickly when we would stop to hand out food, supplies, and Bibles. The pictures below will give you some idea of

the magnitude of the work there.

You may not be able to see it in the last photo but the building has an upper balcony that was also filled with people waiting their turn to come and get a Bible.

Despite the pain registered on the faces of these weeping women, the prayer and worship time would be extremely powerful as people, for so long denied the right to worship in freedom, would raise their voices in unison.

Baptisms, once held in the cover of darkness can now be celebrated in the light of day. These are photos from some of our early baptism services.

Humanitarian Aid

Walk in the Light Ministries provides humanitarian aid in many forms and in many areas of Romania. Often we bring in medical teams that provide free dental care and consultations.

We also support approximately 25 families in the Bistrita and Livezile areas with food and money for utilities. In addition, we employ parents at our facilities, offering them wages and training.

Some families send older children to work instead of school to help make ends meet.

Some families barely make enough money to cover basic expenses and are forced to choose between utilities or rent and food.

These photos were taken at one of the state-run orphanages shortly after the fall of communism in Romania. The building in the background housed over 500 children in sub-standard conditions. The photo on the left shows one of the state-run rooms with blankets and children in warm, colorful clothing. This was the room fixed up to show visiting dignitaries and other guests.

Amy Coroama (in the white shirt below) knows the reality these children lived in. She became separated from the tour group and found herself in the section of the building that was hidden from public view. The children were mostly naked, teens mixed with smaller children. Hungry for food and affection, they literally clawed at her, forcing her into a corner of the room. They were dirty and desperate for attention. Later the group made its way past many rooms filled with infants and toddlers, some suffering from disease, crammed into cribs, living in eerie silence, rocking back and forth. With no one to rock them they had resorted to rocking themselves.

Amy is the wife of Dan Coroama, Ministry Director. A mother of five, she occasionally travels and speaks with Dan, sharing her first-hand experiences of life in Romania as a missionary and

a pastor's wife.

Romania has worked hard since becoming free to affect change in the orphanage system. Most state-run facilities have been closed and the country is moving towards a foster care system.

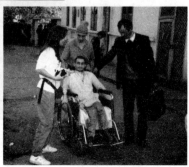

How You Can become Involved With Walk in the Light Ministries

We are looking for dedicated partners to help us rescue as many children as possible. Even though our headquarters is located in the States, we receive prayer, support, and volunteers from around the world.

Walk in the Light (WITL) Ministries relies on the Holy Spirit to move on the hearts of those who wish to help the many suffering children and families of Romania. Prayer is our first and most important request, and we appreciate all the "Prayer Warriors" that intercede on behalf of this ministry. Without help and direction from the Lord, we could do nothing.

WITL also welcomes those who desire to come to Romania to help care for the children, make necessary repairs and maintenance to buildings and equipment, help with planting and harvesting at the farm, and lend their expertise in building additional housing and other structures. Contact the office for further information on upcoming mission trips.

Daniel Coroama, Ministry Director

Daniel Coroama served as pastor for the church that WITL founded in Radauti, Romania, for ten years. In 2002, he returned

to Washington, Missouri with his wife, Amy, and three children, Josiah, Emily, and Matthew to oversee the home office and await the arrival of their fourth child, Laura. This fall, a fifth child, Joshua, was added to their family.

Daniel was 10 years old when he and his mother, brothers, and sisters were told they could leave Romania. As a child, he remembers his father coming home bruised and bleeding from interrogations, and the unspoken rule that you didn't ask what had happened or why his 'Tati' (dad) was beaten again. He can still list the names of relatives and friends who tried to escape Romania and what fate awaited each. He watched the government seize their home and belongings, and give his mother $25.00 as the purchase price.

As an eyewitness to many of the miracles his family has experienced, Dan is a powerful storyteller and speaker, bringing the audience into the scene as he relates his experiences and those of his family.

Daniel is available to speak and share the Gospel and Walk in the Light Ministry with any congregation or group. Call the office to schedule a date or go on-line and submit your request at ilie@yhti.net.

Sam Coroama, Construction Coordinator

Sam was born in 1970 in Romania, the fifth child of Ilie and Aurica. His father escaped from Romania when he was four. Many of his early childhood memories were a blur until returning to Romania in the summer of 1988. This trip set in motion the plans for Sam's life.

In 1990, Sam returned to Romania to help. He translated for mission teams that came to help, passed out Bibles and humanitarian aid. There were so many that needed help, but it was the children that stood out the most. God spoke to his father about starting an orphanage, which would be the first Christian orphanage in the country. Land was purchased and a construction company was hired. After catching the company stealing numerous times, they had to be fired in the middle of the construction process. Sam was asked to take over the project.

Overwhelmed with the responsibility, he accepted and God was faithful to guide his steps. Sam traveled to Vienna, Austria, with $1,500.00 to purchase the tools needed the most, and within less than a year, they were able to move the children into new quarters. Since then, he has overseen all the construction in

Romania, traveling back and forth while maintaining his own construction company in Washington, Missouri.

While completing the second and third house at Livezile, he met one of our orphans and fell in love with her. Sam and Mirela married in December 1997. They returned to the States in July 1998. Sam and Mirela make their home in Washington with their two children, Gabriella and Samuel.

Conny & Lidia Nuebert

Lidia Coroama, born in Romania, still remains there today taking care of our children at the facility in Dornesti. After attending Zion Bible School, she returned to Romania with her family on that original convoy of humanitarian aid after Ceausescu was removed from power.

While there, a man came and knelt in front of her and begged for a Bible. Thin and haggard, his only request was for food for his soul rather than for food for his body. He kissed Lidia's hand in thanks. That moment helped chart the course for the next season of her life. Returning to Romania in 1991, she has used her gift of administration and her love for the children to facilitate care for the orphans and the poor at both the Livezile and Dornesti locations.

Conny arrived at the Dornesti orphanage on a mission trip from Germany. While working on behalf of WITL, he fell in love with Lidia and she with him, and they were married.

Today, they work side by side, managing the Dornesti facility. After a few years of marriage, they decided to begin the proceedings to adopt two beautiful little girls. During that time they were blessed to have a son! Now a family of five, their lives are full and richly blessed.

Towns, Cities, Counties

Berecsaul Mare
(be-rec-so mar-ay)

Banat (bo-naut)

Botosani (bo-to-shaun)

Bucovina (boo-co-ve-na)

Carpenis (car-pen-ish)

Cernauti (cher-noots)

Cluj (cloosh)

Constanta (con-stan-ta)

Dersca (der-es-ca)

Dorohoi (dor-a-hoy)

Dornesti (dor-ne-sht)

Iasi (yash)

Jimbolia (jim-bal-ia)

Moldova (mul-do-va)

Oneaga (o-nee-a-ga)

Oradia (o-ra-dee-a)

Peiding (pee-ding)

Radauti (ra-da-oots)

Sat Chinez (sa-chi-nez)

Siret (see-ret)

Suceava (su-cha-va)

Timis (ti-miss)

Timisoara (ti-me-shar-a)

Triest (trist)

Trischirken (tri-skeer-ken)

Vicov de Jos (vi-coo de jos)

River Bega (bay-ga)

Hotel Coroana de Aur
(cor-a-na-de-our)

Names

Aspazia (es-pas-zea)

Aurica (aw-re-ca)

Ceausescu (chow-ches-coo)

Christu Bab (chre-stu bob)

Doina (do-ee-na)

Florica (flor-ee-ca)

Galan (gay-lan)

Ilie (il-lee)

Iliuta (il-lee-oot-tsa)

Margrethe (mar-gret)

Mihai (me-hi)

Paraschiza (par-a-she-za)

Pavel Balos (pa-vel ba-losh)

Jurzupe (shur-zapa)

Units, Weights, & Measures

15 lei = in that day worth almost $100.00

500 lei = in that day worth approximately 2 weeks salary

1000 lei = in that day worth approximately 1 month salary

2000 lei = in that day worth approximately 3 months salary

2000 lei = after communism worth approximately $25.00

1 meter = .91 yard

2 meters = 1.83 yards

10-15 meters = 9.14-13.72 yards

200 meters = 182.88 yards

1 kilogram = just over 2 pounds

2 kilograms = 4.41 pounds

100 kilometers = 62.14 miles

250 kilometers = 155.35 miles

250-300 kilometers = 155.35-186.42 miles

3000 Deutsch marks = worth approxiamtely $2,000 on today's market

Romania

- International boundary
- County (judeţ) boundary
- ★ National capital
- ◉ County (judeţ) center

Bucureşti is a municipality (municipiu).

- Railroad
- Expressway
- Road

0 25 50 75 100 Kilometers
0 25 50 75 100 Miles

Lambert Conformal Conic Projection, SP 40N/56N

Serbia and Montenegro have asserted the formation of a joint independent state, but this entity has not been formally recognized as a state by the United States.

Base 802205 (R01144) 5-96

183

Walk In the Light Ministries

PO BOX 1516 ▶ Washington, MO 63090

Phone: 636-239-9409 ▶ Fax:636-239-0790

www.redeemthetime.com

· A *higher standard.*
A *higher purpose.*

Walk in the Light is a member in good standing with the ECFA. All contributions are tax-deductible and are used as specified.

Contributions to the on-going mission of Walk in the Light Ministries may be mailed to our office at the address above or you may make donations using credit cards by visiting our website.

Additional copies of this book are available for a donation. Please contact the Walk in the Light Ministries office at the address above. You may also order this book online at www.redeemthetime.com.

Thank you for helping us help the children
and the poor of Romania.
May God richly bless you.
From the staff of *Walk in the Light Ministries*